SERVING THE UNEMPLOYED

and their families

robert **SUNLEY** &
g. william **SHEEK**

Family Service America
Milwaukee

Family Service America

11700 West Lake Park Drive, Milwaukee, WI 53224

Library of Congress Cataloging-in-Publication Data

Sunley, Robert, 1917-
Serving the unemployed and their families.

Bibliography: p.
1. Family social work--United States. 2. Unemployed--Services for--United States. 3. Unemployment--Social aspects--United States. I. Sheek, G. William, 1936- . II. Title.
HV699.S86 1986 362.8'5'0973 86-6344
ISBN 0-87304-218-2

Printed in the United States of America

3

CONTENTS

PREFACE

Unemployment is both a challenging and fluctuating problem within our society. And elusive as a solution to the problem is, there is an undisputed "bottom line" of unemployment. Those who are unemployed experience tremendous emotional and resource upheaval which eventually affects their families.

It was with sensitivity to the devastating effects of unemployment that the National Academy for Families invited Family Service America (the primary direct service family organization in the U.S.) to collaborate in producing a resource designed to assist in upgrading existing services and/or in creating new means of serving unemployed clients and families.

This publication (the end product of this collaboration) was funded and facilitated by NAF with guidance from FSA. It reflects learnings gleaned from surveying FSA member agencies, in-depth follow-ups to numerous agencies and a conference of selected agencies with intensive services for the unemployed.

We now have much information to share from the experiences of agencies which have been most effective in serving unemployed clients and families. And it is the hope of NAF and FSA that the information in this publication will encourage your agency toward increased service on behalf of the unemployed. We know it contains guidelines essential to that direction.

Many persons and agencies deserve credit for their unique and essential contributions to this publication. Here are the major ones:

Lydia and John S. Schweppe, M.D. for their unremitting concern for families and for their commitment to and generosity in funding national family-serving organizations, including the National Academy for Families. It was under the auspices of NAF that this book was developed and written.

The board of directors and advisory committee of NAF for their administrative support.

Robert Sunley for his experience with, insights about, and commitment to families suffering from unemployment--all reflected in his co-authorship of this book.

Robert Rice and the staff of Family Service America for encouragement, cooperation, expertise, and hard work.

The staff and executives of the many FSA member agencies who responded to the survey, conference, and in-depth follow-up, allowing valuable information on behalf of unemployed clients and families to be shared with the readers.

Grant Loavenbruck for assistance in research design and data analysis.

J. Ann Craig, assistant to the Executive Director of NAF, for her support-staff contributions.

G. William Sheek
Executive Director
National Academy for Families

1

UNEMPLOYMENT AND ITS IMPACT

National figures on unemployment tend to diffuse the real impact of unemployment even in relatively good times. The statistics deal with averages for the entire country; they do not reveal the conditions of the lives of vast numbers of people who dwell in places where the rate of joblessness far exceeds the national average.

Although the national unemployment rate may have declined to about 7 percent from the peak of more than 10 percent in the recession period of 1981-82, some areas still report rates ranging to 11 or 12 percent. In some states, such as Michigan, the rate has been higher than the national average for over two years. The higher rates in Michigan prevail primarily in geographical and occupational areas related to the auto industry.

In addition to regional pockets of joblessness, the nation suffers from the unemployment that strikes individual communities when major industries close down or cut back the operations of local plants. Such loss of jobs is extremely serious for a city or town. An improved national employment average is little solace for the people of an afflicted community; their needs are pressing and immediate.

A third factor in the ongoing unemployment situation is the increase in "structural" unemployment caused by changes in technology and other critical production forces. Not only may large plants close down, an entire industry may undergo a major transition. People with many years of tenure in a given factory or a particular industry suddenly find themselves jobless, with skills that are obsolete, often at an age when reemployment is unlikely.

The extent of structural unemployment can be judged from data released by the federal government covering the years 1979-84. Out of a total of 11.5 million persons who became unemployed, 5.1 million had at least three year's tenure; that is, they had worked steadily for that length of time. The balance of 6.4 million had shorter job tenure.

It is instructive to know what happened to the 5.1 million workers who became unemployed through shutdowns or staff cuts. New jobs were found by 3.1 million, but of these, 900,000 had to accept pay cuts, 500,000 of them cuts exceeding 20 percent. Of the remainder, 1.3 million were still looking for work at the time of the study, and 700,000 had dropped out of the work force. Of those who found new jobs, it should be noted that in the twenty- to twenty-four-year-old group, 70 percent found new jobs but in the fifty-five to sixty-four-year-old group, only 41 percent did.

The impact of unemployment is strikingly uneven. Some groups are little affected while others are hit hard. For example, in 1982 the unemployment rate among black teenagers was 46.7 percent in contrast to 7.6 percent for married men whose spouses were living with them.[1]

Still further disparities are seen: For example, the impact on different groups is important, in that younger single workers may have a somewhat higher rate of unemployment but suffer far less stress than middle-aged workers with dependent families. The length of unemployment and the availability of assets and other resources are also critical factors and vary with different population groups. The impact of unemployment is softened if a person is affiliated with a union and if there are prospects for reemployment locally.

The effect of unemployment differs greatly among individual families. Some unemployed quickly find new jobs at comparable pay and most feel little lasting distress. Others eventually get jobs within a year and still others either drop out of the labor market or continue looking.

MAJOR CONSEQUENCES

There are five major consequences that people suffer because of unemployment. Some families are burdened by all of them; others may experience only one or two, albeit very painfully. The consequences are loss of savings, loss of home, loss of medical insurance, more health problems, increased stress, and mental health difficulties.

Loss of Savings

Families may have to exhaust savings built up over years of good earnings. Savings are supposed to be for a "rainy day," and when they are gone, the family feels helpless. Homeowners find they cannot make needed major repairs; because they are unemployed, they may not be able to borrow for this purpose, and, if they can borrow, they cannot afford to repay a loan. This lack of any financial reserve is particularly frightening to those who had foreseen the need for resources of their own. Accepting a job at lower pay may mean their inability to continue or resume savings, so that psychological and financial security is removed. Quite a few see themselves at the brink of welfare and become increasingly anxious. These feelings of inadequacy may make it harder to seek and find employment.

Loss of Home

With their savings gone and with an inadequate unemployment insurance income, many families face the possibility of foreclosure of the mortgages on their homes. Others, although not homeowners, may have trouble paying rent or may have their cars or other valued and needed possessions repossessed. While banks or other financial institutions may sometimes be patient with an unemployed homeowner with a good record of employment and of mortgage payments, the homeowner can foresee serious trouble as he or she comes to the end of even the unemployment insurance. Sometimes families ward off the worst possibilities because one member has been able to find a job or continue working; nonetheless, total family income may be considerably lower than needed.

Loss of Medical Insurance

Effects on health care are potentially complex. One obvious difficulty is the loss of medical insurance based on prior employment. Although most medical insurance provides that a person can continue the insurance by paying individually, this usually provides much less coverage at higher cost; one estimate is that the cost might run as high as 60 percent of the unemployment check. About 61 percent of the U.S. population is covered by medical insurance either through employment of self or a family member; the extent of coverage varies both regionally and by race, with only about 50 percent of blacks and Hispanics covered. The lapse of medical insurance leads the unemployed to postpone health care, routine health needs, and to sacrifice other needs when health care is essential.

More Health Problems

The direct effects of unemployment on personal health have been studied; while adverse effects are not uniform, there is a definite correlation between joblessness and increased ill-health. The study by

M. Harvey Brenner of Johns Hopkins University showed that, with the increase of 1 percent in unemployment, there were increases of 4.1 percent in suicides, of 5.7 percent in homicides, of 1.9 percent in deaths from heart disease, liver cirrhosis, and stress-related disorders, and of 2 to 4 percent in hospital admissions. Other data indicate that nutritional deficiencies increase with unemployment and pregnant women are affected especially. An increase in infant mortality was noted in Michigan, where persisting unemployment has led to long-term problems for many people.

Increased Stress

Family life is subjected to stress when a family member is unemployed. People in certain family life stages are more severely affected than others. For example, families with preschoolers tend to have wage earners with relatively less experience and job tenure and with fewer resources for coping with adversity. Hence, they are more vulnerable to stresses that impinge adversely upon very young children through their distraught parents. Families with older adolescents about to enter college may have to economize; the youth may have to go to work to help the family survive. This seems to happen often because of the stress-related illnesses of one or both parents--illnesses that threaten the prospects of returning to work. Beyond such phase-specific consequences of unemployment, the overall stresses are well known: increases in family disharmony; conflict between parents; increases in family violence; alcoholism and drug abuse. While no studies are known to the authors, they conjecture that the effects of such stresses persist in many families after unemployment ends.

Mental Health Difficulties

The effects of unemployment on mental health have been described frequently. Individuals often experience losses of self-esteem, of some aspects of functioning, of support networks, and of the sources of rewards and social gratifications. Some unemployed workers are depressed, preoccupied with suicide or physically aggressive; anxiety attacks are common. Behavioral manifestations include feelings of weakness, tiredness, excessive sleeping or sleep disturbances, inability to perform routine chores, overeating, withdrawing from social contacts and watching television excessively, and neglecting personal care and appearance. Many such persons do not seek mental health services, but instead look for help for somatic complaints or financial or family problems. They tend to be distracted from looking for work. Their individual problems, rooted in hidden psychological factors, may go unattended.

Many unemployed people suffer severe grief reactions because they have lost their jobs and go through the stages of bereavement. They are often unable to work out the loss over a reasonable period of time and thus suffer ongoing symptoms of depression. Others are precipitated into ill-advised actions during the period of mourning; for example, in grieving, one phase involves the urge to search for or replace what was lost, and some unemployed may find themselves moving hurriedly to another city or area of the country in an effort to find work at once--although economically and for other reasons, the move should be delayed or not made at all.

The complex and far-reaching effects of unemployment underscore the gravity of the problem. The consequences are particularly burdensome to certain population groupings, notably blacks and other minorities and single women maintaining households. Generally our society has made grievously inadequate responses to unemployment. Unemployment insurance is insufficient and short-lived, and the welfare system, which is the last fallback position for the unemployed, often further deepens the effects of unemployment. Apart from strictly financial supports, many other kinds of help are needed.

This chapter's discussion of unemployment and its impact is brief, intended primarily to provide introductory background to the book's presentation of the findings of a study and the implications of these findings. More detailed information about unemployment's effect on people may be found in Appendexes 1 and 2.

REFERENCE

1. See Appendix 1.

2

UNEMPLOYMENT AND FAMILIES: A SURVEY

In early 1984, the National Academy for Families (NAF) and Family Service America (FSA) embarked on a joint study of unemployment as seen by family service agencies in the United States. The national organizations particularly wanted to determine what services had been provided by the agencies in 1983 in response to the severe recession that had started in 1981. More precisely, the study sought to discover what the agencies did as part of their regular practice and what they did as special projects to meet the pressing needs of the unemployed and their families.

The results of the survey are significant and have permanent value. Perhaps the most important conclusion that may be drawn is that unemployment is a permanent rather than an occasional problem. In the United States, at any time of the year, a large number of people are unemployed. Many of them and many of their family members suffer serious consequences.

The survey went out to member agencies of Family Service America in the United States, at that time about 220 agencies. A total of 188 responded, of which one-third, or sixty-eight, indicated that some special project or allocation of service had been made in 1983 to better assist the unemployed. Many agencies, in addition to completing the survey form, also sent the researchers copies of materials they had used to help the unemployed and to inform the media of their activities.

One of the main purposes of the survey was to find out what services other than those usually offered were made available, under what auspices, and with what funding. Other significant information was sought through questions such as these:

What proportion of regular clients coming to family agencies had problems connected with unemployment?

Did special projects for the unemployed actually reach such people?

What sectors of our society seemed to be cooperative in working on the problems of the unemployed?

What part did clinical services play in helping the unemployed?

What kinds of problems seem to be most related to unemployment?

How were collaborative efforts among organizations initiated?

What kinds of services were needed, in addition to clinical and family life education, and how did communities move to meet these service needs?

The survey was designed to elicit answers to these and similar questions, using a form (see Appendix 3) organized in five categories:

A. Community information: rate of unemployment, organizations, including unions, providing assistance, and the degree of cooperation or resistance encountered.

B. Agency information: an overall view of size of caseload, income levels of clients, allocations of staff time among services, advocacy efforts.

C. Daily routine practice of the agency: how agencies handled applicants with problems related to unemployment, most common problems, most needed services other than clinical, what types of situations were referred out and where, and related aspects.

D. General questions: opinions as to most important current and future issues related to unemployment.

E. Special service projects: whether a community coalition was formed, role of agency in it, funding sources, use of consultants, agency estimates of outcomes of special services, media materials and recognition, and related points.

An overall purpose of the survey was to collect information that could be used to prepare for future unemployment problems at the community level and the local agency level. The scope of the findings thus goes beyond relevance for a local agency to significance in community planning for human needs.

THE FINDINGS

The findings of the survey are reported in this chapter under the headings corresponding to the five main sections of the questionnaire.

Community Information

Although the rates of unemployment in their communities ranged from 4 to 20 percent, most agencies reported rates from around 10 to 14 percent. Their approximations were fairly close to the national average for much of 1983. But the impact of unemployment is poorly conveyed by such figures. In some communities, the drastic cutback in a work force or the closing down of a major enterprise had a most severe effect on both those immediately thrown out of work and also on other people whose earnings or businesses were related to or dependent on the depressed industry.

Analysis of answers to the survey showed that, in general, communities responded to such crises in a heartening way. The community organizations identified as most effective in helping the unemployed were primarily the governmental agencies set up for that purpose: the state employment agencies, the departments of social service, colleges and universities for training purposes, and local groups and agencies for such immediate needs as food, fuel, and shelter.

Contrary to what might have been expected, agencies found relatively little resistance to collaborative work to help the unemployed among the various community organizations. Over 80 percent of the agencies responding on this point rated the collaboration on the positive side. The balance encountered problems of territorial jealousy or resistant attitudes.

In general, responses about the attitudes and helpfulness of the labor unions were quite positive; reports indicated that some offered cash assistance, information and referral, outreach, and workshops. The labor representatives on the local United Ways were mentioned as being particularly helpful.

Perhaps the most important conclusion that can be reached from these findings is that, in most communities, there is a large, cooperative pool of various kinds of helping services; these services, however, need to be better coordinated in planning and developing programs for the unemployed now and in the future. Ongoing coalitions of this type may also prove more effective in stimulating support and participation from large corporations, which, according to survey results, seem for the most part to have little if any involvement in helping the unemployed.

Agency Information

The average agency served 3,000 clients in a year; most clients had annual incomes under \$15,000. There was, however, considerable variation among agencies; a few had a high percentage of high-income clients, and a few had almost all low-income clients. These differences in incomes may have resulted in disparities among agencies in the ways they served the unemployed. However, the survey results show that the recession hit people in all income brackets--not, as usually thought, only low-income earners.

The survey sought to learn what proportions of staff time were spent on the major types of services and in turn what proportions of staff time went to the unemployed. Because of variations, the findings can be expressed only in ranges. As might be expected, the great bulk of paid staff time went into clinical services, and a relatively small percentage of such clinical service time went to helping the unemployed. (A somewhat different perspective will be given in the next section in relation to caseloads.) Family life educational services were allocated a much smaller percentage of agency staff time, and advocacy the least.

The concentration on clinical services reflects the findings described earlier: such services are the major offering of agencies generally and are usually seen by them as their most effective contribution to a community-wide effort to grapple with unemployment.

What little proportion of staff time was spent in advocacy was consumed primarily by case advocacy, and presumably was often done in connection with rendering concrete services. In a later chapter, the role of advocacy in preparing and developing services for the unemployed will be taken up in more detail. For the moment, it is sufficient to observe that advocacy was less needed on the case level than might be expected, owing to the relatively high degree of cooperation obtained from other community agencies in helping the unemployed.

Routine Daily Practices of the Agency

Taken on the average, out of a caseload of 3,000 a year, about 23 percent of the clients had problems engendered by unemployment. Because of the difficulties of definition and the complexities of obtaining data, the findings can best be viewed as suggesting that a fairly substantial number of people suffered from the effects of unemployment, either their own or that of a family member.

Agencies were asked to determine the most common clinical problems and other service needs engendered by unemployment. Such information is highly important in pointing to the relevance of clinical services and to the needs for other types of services both by an agency and by other community groups.

The most common clinical problems were personal (such as stress, depression, and anxiety), family tensions, role adjustment, and alcohol abuse. (A later chapter on clinical services will provide further details.)

Nonclinical service needs having their source in unemployment include the following, listed in order of frequency of being reported in the survey:

Financial counseling
Financial assistance

Job referral and placement
Stress management
Job search skills
Community resource assistance
Redefining vocational goals
Retraining assistance
Assistance in securing entitlements, benefits

Most of the agencies in the survey provided few of these services. Many clients with such service needs were seen in clinical services, presumably mainly for their clinical problems. Education in skills of stress management and job search is a type of service fairly closely related to clinical or educational services which many agencies offered on a group basis. It is discussed later in this chapter.

The extent to which agencies handle cases themselves or refer them to other community helpers is greatly varied, depending on available in-agency services and community services. The desirability of having more nonclincial services available within an agency was made clear: Many agencies indicated the need for support groups, support services, and job-related services.

The information on referrals shows that agencies used a wide variety of community resources. The survey itself did not deal with the effectiveness of the referral process nor the effectiveness of the receiving agency; this type of information is rarely available. In follow-up discussions, it was learned that the capability of community agencies varied widely, depending on such factors as funding, staffing, attitudes, and intake policies. For example, financial counseling may be provided by consumer credit counseling services. These agencies are organized, however, to help people with regular income pay off their debts. Although some credit counseling agencies may try to help persons who, because of unemployment, are without much income, other such agencies may not be able to help or to relate their services to this somewhat different need. Some are not geared to help with bankruptcies, although this service and resolution of financial problems may be necessary for some unemployed people.

An overall assessment of the major service needs which the agencies believed required more of their direct attention shows that advocacy, financial counseling, and outreach to the unemployed ranked highest. All of these are services that most agencies could carry out with funding, staffing, and training--assuming they were not provided by other local agencies. Stress management also ranks high. Job-related services, such as job search skills and job referral, are probably somewhat further removed from the usual agency area of expertise, so that a lower priority would be given to them as an in-agency function. Some of the agencies surveyed, however, ventured into these areas.

The survey also elicited agency evaluation of needed agency-support services. Overall, agencies saw that further staff training, consultation, program development assistance and research were needed.

Agencies were asked to evaluate outcomes of their work with the unemployed: this is, of course, a complex matter. On the average, agencies assisted regular clients (not those in special projects for the unemployed) in getting jobs at the rate of about seventy-three in a year; fifty were helped in securing trainng or retraining. The average is skewed because of several variables; for example, some agencies focused on the unemployed while others did not.

If we take the average agency, with a yearly caseload of 3,000 and with 23 percent of that total persons with problems engendered by unemployment, we find that the agency helped about 20 percent (of the 23 percent) to secure jobs or training. Obviously, this is only one type of measurement of effectiveness. It does not take into account that others among the clients got jobs on their own or through other sources.

Another indicator of results may be sought in staff opinion about agency effectiveness in responding to the needs of the unemployed. The results are not clear, however. About 43 percent of the staff people saw their agency as being of some help; 43 percent saw the help as "minimal," and the balance of 14 percent did not see it as helpful. The survey question appears to have been too general to elicit more meaningful answers, but it would appear that the evaluations reflect the tendency of staff people to undervalue their effectiveness in helping clients. Obviously, the agencies were not set up to provide a maximum array of effective services to unemployed persons. These evaluations relate to regular clients who usually came for personal or family problems.

General Questions

The survey asked agencies to list the most central present issues related to their efforts to serve individuals and families affected by unemployment. The issues were, in order:

1. Neither jobs nor training are available
2. Clients fail to seek help in time or at all
3. Lack of funds for programs
4. Clients' feelings of depression and helplessness
5. Clients cannot afford program fees

Other issues included family breakdown and family violence and needs for medical services, outreach, and appropriate staff.

A corollary question on issues in the next five years was posed, with the following results:

1. Need for funds
2. Lack of jobs
3. Family breakdown
4. Training (for staff, for clients)
5. Coordination with business

Combined with other survey responses, these responses point to important directions for the future for human service agencies relative to unemployment. These directions are explored further in the chapters on advocacy, planning, and the future.

Social Service Projects

One section of the survey focused on special projects, defining them as being primarily for the unemployed and conducted either by one agency or a coalition of agencies.

Special projects tended to be separately funded and conducted regularly through the year. However, quite a few offered one service, such as a job support group which met for a specific number of sessions and was repeated periodically. Generally, the special projects offered one or more of the following: counseling for individuals and families, job information and referral, stress management training, educational and support groups, and emergency assistance.

Roughly 55 percent of the projects were intitated as part of the effort of a community coalition. The members of such coalitions usually were the United Way, legal services, and private health and welfare agencies, including sectarian and ethnic groups. Unions frequently involved included the AFL-CIO, Teamsters, International Brotherhood of Electrical Workers, UAW, Steelworkers, and Foodworkers. Church groups were participants, although perhaps not as many as possible. Corporations played relatively little part, although scattered local assistance came from several national corporations.

Coalitions were most often organized by family agency staff, by labor representatives active in the United Way, or by other United Way staff. In addition to services to the unemployed, agency staffs contributed to the effectiveness of the coalitions by helping with planning and development, coordinating service, and bringing in coalition members.

The special projects served a range of unemployed people, among them the newly laid-off, long-term unemployed, executives never before laid off, those about to be laid off, women heads of households, blue-collar male heads of households, unskilled workers, and older workers.

Significantly, this broad diversity, representing many kinds of problems, led the agencies to obtain much outside expert help from such sources as unions, businesses, and government. The areas of expertise included organization of job clubs; budgeting and financial counseling; resume-writing and career counseling; labor and personnel information; welfare, legal, and social policy; mental health; and entitlements. Many of these were areas of knowledge in which agency staff had had little or no experience. Almost all the agencies with special projects utilized outside help, pointing again to a surprisingly high degree of cooperation from some segments of the community.

Funding for special projects was not high, and additional funds tended to come from the United Way or through allocations from the agency or its immediate supporters. Here and there, agencies obtained grants, government funding, and allocations from religious groups; some funding came through the coalitions rather than directly to the agency.

The outcomes of the special projects were rated higher than the outcomes of the regular service programs. About two-thirds (66 percent) rated the projects as effective, and about one-third "minimally" effective. On the average, the projects helped thirty-six persons to obtain jobs and twenty-one to secure training. However, the data are not adequate to compare with the "regular" service results in regard to such factors as time and type of result. It does appear, however, that, overall, the agencies regarded the projects as very worthwhile and that some achieved considerable successes.

Agencies listed the following elements as necessary to make special projects more helpful: an information clearinghouse on techniques and program development, coordination of local agencies, program development staff, effective publicity, coordination with businesses, and programs for chronically unemployed youth.

ACTIVITIES AFTER THE SURVEY

In the spring of 1984, a conference following up the survey was held to look further into some aspects of unemployment. Participants included staff members of Family Service America and the National Academy for Families, two consultants, and executive directors or senior staff members from six agencies involved in the survey who were from large urban centers.

Although the survey results had not yet been processed, the conference focused on both some of the hands-on experience obtained by several agencies and on technical assistance which was or would be needed in the areas of clinical services, educational services, concrete services, advocacy, and integration and implementation of services.

The goals of FSA in cosponsoring this conference

and the survey were set forth in a 1984 statement by its Board of Directors to:

> "give priority attention to the issue of unemployment throughout the program planning process for 1984-85, including:
>
> 1. Defining activities which may effectively utilize family service agencies to provide direct or preventive services for unemployed families
>
> 2. Providing technical assistance to FSA member agencies to carry out such tasks
>
> 3. Monitoring governmental activities regarding unemployment as they affect families and family life
>
> 4. Implementing education and advocacy activities nationally in behalf of unemployed families"[1]

Services for helping the unemployed were identified in four categories: clinical, educational, concrete, and advocacy. These are reflected in the preceding discussion of the survey and its findings. Technical assistance was defined as "the mobilization of special knowledge and technical resources for initiating, increasing the effectiveness of, and integrating services on behalf of the client families of unemployed."

The substance of the conference is reflected throughout this book in a number of general ways. There were several conclusions that should be mentioned specifically. They reflect the experience of agencies actively involved in programs for the unemployed and reveal the concern of the agencies and the urgency and complexity that are characteristic of helping the unemployed. They are:

- Motivation of unemployed persons is important.

- Accessing employment--for example, through social networks, cooperative job searching, and contacts with industry--is vital.

- The Job Partnership Training Act (JPTA) has not been very effective or helpful in local agency projects.

- Unions are sometimes interested in helping, sometimes not. Retraining may be viewed by labor as a threat to dues-paying members.

- Private Industry Councils (PICs) are weak on advocacy and political involvement.

- People who are "new poor" and those who are "old poor" involve different issues. Recently unemployed ("new poor") are often angrier. The chronically unemployed ("old poor") must not be ignored in this recent heightened interest in the employment plight of the industrial sector.

- Keep focus on "all the people" so that some groups are not overlooked--such as women and minorities who suffer from the "last hired, first fired" syndrome.

- Agencies may have limits (small staff and clinical emphasis, for example) that must be recognized when unemployment programs are planned.

- An agency's board of directors, advisers, and executives need to be involved if the agency is to address local unemployment issues effectively.

- Unemployment issues are bringing agencies back to the roots of social work through the need for concrete education and advocacy services.

- Staff people need to address both concrete and clinical issues, including the questioning of male-female roles when unemployment demands a shift in traditional patterns.

- Self-help is sometimes threatening to the clinician, but it is vital when the concerns of the unemployed are addressed.

- Coalescing of social service organizations helps meet the varied needs of the unemployed.

- Funding is a problem because the clients, by definition, are unable to pay for services. Perhaps unemployee assistance programs could be sold to corporations.

- Timing of intervention programs for clients is important. Although people tend to be uninterested in support programs until their income (as distinct from their pay) and entitlements run out, assistance can be helpful much before then. Grieving stages are applicable in the loss of a job and may provide clues as to the best timing for offering services.

- Marketing and public relations are important. Potential closings need to be identified. Unemployment fluctuates, which makes it difficult to set up an established program.

- It is not easy to program around unemployment when so much government money and public relations are going into selling the public an economic recovery.

In addition to the conference, telephone follow-up was used to contact a number of agencies to elicit more detail on various points covered summarily by the survey. The results are discussed in following chapters, particularly the one on model programs. The agencies were selected for follow-up on the basis that each had conducted an effective service or services for the unemployed. Their programs exemplified various sources of funding, staffing patterns, and degrees of community linkage and coalition building.

Overall, these follow-up contacts indicate that the major problem in coping with large numbers of unemployed in a sharp recession is community-wide lack of funding. In 1983, many agencies had for the first time faced considerable unemployment among suburban residents, people who had been working steadily for years and who had seemed relatively safe from the ups and downs of the economy. A somewhat parallel group was also noticeable: a large number of urban unemployed who had risen somewhat above the poverty level, had worked steadily, and believed themselves far enough ahead to not fear falling back into poverty and all that it can mean. Minorities, and particularly blacks, found themselves in this predicament, since they were often the "last hired, first fired." This added de facto discrimination to the brutal experience of being laid off.

The results of the survey, then, should always be seen in the light of the great personal, emotional impact of joblessness if they are to be valuable in planning for future responses to unemployment.

3

CLINICAL AND OTHER SERVICES

Out of the 188 agencies that responded to the survey, one-third had a special project or service that focused on the unemployed. All the agencies reported that, on the average, about 23 percent of their caseloads involved persons with problems engendered by unemployment; thus, the two-thirds that did not have special projects nonetheless provided clinical services to people presenting problems related to unemployment. Since clinical counseling services represent the greatest part of the agencies' total services, and in most communities their particular expertise, a further analysis of the provision of clinical services is indicated.

The most common clinical problems or complaints caused by unemployment were reported to be, in order of frequency:

Personal (such as stress, depression, anxiety, lower self-esteem, grief, anger, blame, and confusion)
Family (tension and breakdown, other than the above)
Role adjustments
Alcohol abuse
Spouse abuse
Child abuse
Drug abuse
Relocation or separation
Suicidal tendencies

The agencies provided services to most of those persons who had problems that fell in the first three categories. They tended to refer out quite a substantial portion of persons presenting other types of problems, especially alcohol and drug abuse. In many cases, the agencies provided some services to a person and referred others. Generally, it appears that persons needing help were primarily served within the overall programs of the agencies. The intake or assessment interviews at the point of initial contacts with a person seemed to function well, in that most persons presenting problems related to unemployment were informed of services elsewhere that more directly related to problems stemming specifically from unemployment.

Clinical services are those of individual, marital, and family counseling, involving one or more family members and concerned primarily with reactions, conflicts, and disturbances. Agency educational services and advocacy services are distinct from clinical services. So are such specific helping activities as financial counseling; assistance obtaining fuel, food, and housing; and assistance with such job-centered activities as setting vocational goals, obtaining job retraining, and developing job search skills.

At the point of intake, then, agencies differentiated among the problems and the service responses. The survey helped indicate not only the responses but the gaps in services experienced by the agencies in trying to meet needs. The primary lacks in clinical services appeared to be, first, the need for increased funding and, second, the need for staff training.

Agency educational programs seemed to be the most directly correlated with clinical services, particularly in the form of groups interested in stress management and job search skills. Both subjects lend themselves particularly well to group process and also appeal to many who do not see the need for individual or family counseling.

Agencies with special projects for the unemployed also focused in much the same way on counseling and educational services. However, as noted later, they also set up other services. The survey responses and the follow-up discussions revealed that the variations in the agencies' responses to the problems of the unemployed generally depended on such factors as the availability of services in the community, the practicality of diverting staff time, and the possibility of new funding.

The relevance of clinical services to the problems and complaints of the jobless may be seen in the description of a typical unemployed client that appears in "Serving the Unemployed," the journal article that is Appendix 1 in this book. In addition to symptoms of poor physical health, the person feels depressed, frightened, and hopeless. The same article offers the valuable insight that a person who has lost his or her job feels the loss as a bereavement and suffers the same reactions that are felt by someone who has lost a loved one to death. The article points out that the reactions may be present "individually, successively, or collectively."

Thus, clinical services, in addition to individual counseling in which such grief reactions can be handled, might well use group approaches; bereavement groups have proved helpful to those distressed by the death of a spouse or other family member. Clinical judgments are clearly necessary to determine which clients might benefit from such groups, and which might not be helped, for a variety of reasons.

Although the survey did not determine the extent

to which family therapy or family interviews are used with the unemployed, we know from the experiences of some agencies that this approach can also be helpful. One frequent need for involvement of family members is to strengthen the unemployed person's support network. Studies have shown that eventually (usually sooner than later) a support network begins to weaken, and even family members withdraw support. Worse yet, the atmosphere of blame and reproach, whether or not directly voiced by others, further depresses the unemployed person.

Finally, individual determinations must be made as to the relative weights of past psychological and family problems as against the effects of the current situation. For example, do the presenting symptoms primarily indicate a situational or reactive depression or the exacerbation of already existing symptoms and problems? Obviously, referring some persons to direct, job-related services without a course of counseling may be quite ineffective. Whether or not the agency provides other services in addition to clinical services, the agency stands as a provider of a critical service for many unemployed, that of differential diagnosis and assessment of a spectrum of possible service needs.

OTHER TYPES OF SERVICE

The survey revealed that, in addition to clinical services, agencies responded to unemployment in their communities with programs of advocacy and education, as well as specific services. The agency actions were determined in part because of the presence or absence of existing community services or the ability of other organizations to provide one or more such services.

Generally, agencies regarded certain services as being more appropriate for them to undertake than others. Direct, job-related services were seen by them as being least suitable; they considered educational groups and advocacy to be closer to their usual functions.

Seven types of services were reported:

Information and Referral (I & R)

This type of service was carried out in one or more of three ways: by written materials such as directories of community resources; by telephone; and by group meetings in which I & R was one feature. Many communities published directories of services relevant to the unemployed, often under United Way auspices but also sponsored by individual agencies, unions, religious groups, and other organizations. The distribution of special I & R directories presumably was seen as meeting a widespread need, although no figures were submitted or obtained to show the extent of the need. Such directories convey better than any other single means the remarkable pulling together of resources in communities across the country to help the unemployed. Many agencies had already been providing I & R to applicants, although not necessarily in a separate, unemployment-related, service. They usually did it in intake interviews.

Information and referral can be provided at several levels. The first level is simply that of information on resources, including eligibility and contact telephone numbers. Such information is often printed as well as being given over the telephone. Although a valuable service, it is often not sufficient: The next level is that of a responsive service, in which a person staffs the service to field more specific questions, give information, and make referrals. Finally, the referral itself is treated as an important service, and the staff endeavors to involve an applicant sufficiently to determine underlying or additonal needs, erroneous perceptions of problems and resources, and possible conflicting motives that could hinder the use of resources. A number of agency survey responses indicated the provision of this further service.

Concrete Services

There were many types, among them food banks (collections of food, usually donated, to be given away); food vouchers (for use at local supermarkets); soup kitchens; clothing and appliances (usually donated); shelter; small cash grants for specific needs including food, transportation, or shelter. Overall, the survey indicated that agencies did not play a major role in the provision of such services in most communities. Where coalitions existed, the agency tended to provide one such service at most, or to take part in helping. One agency, for example, conducted sensitivity training for volunteers working in a soup kitchen. Sectarian community organizations took on the responsibility for much of the provision of concrete services, usually as an extension or continuation of work they had been already doing.

While counseling agencies tend not to regard provision of concrete services as appropriate or desirable for them, the survey and follow-ups indicated that many of the unemployed are not reached by and do not want counseling, but do recognize and respond to the provision of basic needs. Whether this leads them to become involved in counseling is not clear from the survey. Conjecturally, some will go on to counseling, just as some who come for counseling need concrete services; the progression needs to be made by the clients as they recognize and want help.

Financial Help

One of the most frequently needed services, according to the survey, was financial counseling. This term usually includes budgeting, money management, debt counseling, and assistance with mortgage payments. Most human service agencies do not have staff with expertise in these matters, and common sense only goes part of the way in helping someone cope with such problems. In many larger communities, consumer credit counseling services function as nonprofit organizations helping the heavily indebted. Most are supported, however, by creditors and tend to be able to help those who are working and have earnings that make repayment of debts feasible. They are not specifically geared to helping the unemployed, especially persons in long-term unemployment, or to help with bankruptcy when that may be the only humane recourse for the family. Several of the responding agencies developed financial counseling services, usually in areas which lacked a consumer credit counseling service. They emphasized helping lower income people and a more comprehensive approach to the family in financial trouble. The services tend to operate with a mixture of paid staff and trained volunteers.

One agency with a financial counseling program separated the granting of any direct financial assistance into a different service which responds to crises, mainly of the poor. This separation helps avoid the problem of some applicants for financial counseling seeking the repayment of debts by the agency, thus solving their financial problems. While for the most part cash grants made by agencies are small, occasional needs arise for larger amounts: for example, making up the balance of funds for obtaining a place to live, right away; or equipping oneself and getting to a promised job. Where community coalitions exist, provision can be made to assign this type of financial assistance to one or more agencies, separate from financial counseling.

Financial counseling, budgeting, and money management were frequently handled in group sessions for the unemployed. These sessions were usually called "Coping with Unemployment" or something similar. Again, as with I & R services, several levels of help may be indicated.

Advocacy

About 15 percent of the agencies responding to the survey carried out advocacy in regard to the unemployed; this was mostly case advocacy. One of the lacks mentioned by many agencies, however, was the capability to provide advocacy services for the unemployed. There were indications from the survey and the follow-ups that somewhat more advocacy did go on at the community level. This was suggested by the descriptions of certain services initiated (though not carried out) by agencies, such as arranging health care for unemployed or helping a group provide day care.

Groups/Family Life Education

A variety of groups were conducted around the general theme of coping with unemployment. Some were concerned with stress management and some with coping with personal reactions to unemployment. Others dealt with family financial concerns, job clubs and networks, and combinations of these topics. While job clubs tended to be of a self-help nature, most groups were conducted by agency staff. Usually, they met for a specified number of weekly sessions. Promotional materials announcing the groups usually appealed to the need of the unemployed for information and for discussing employment-related problems. Most tried to "normalize" unemployment, instilling the attitude that the individual was one among many with the same problem and emphasizing that seeking help was the right thing to do. (Figures 1-3 show typical materials.)

Group meetings were generally held on agency premises, though some were in quarters belonging to unions, religious institutions, and places of business. (The latter were sometimes used by employees being laid off.)

Figure 1

UNEMPLOYED?

- You're not alone and you don't have to face problems alone.
- Child and Family Services is bringing together unemployed workers to talk and find solutions to their needs such as:

Fighting boredom	Job retraining
Stretching budgets	Family problems
Relocation	Buffalo's job future

- Small groups will meet once a week at various locations. This free program, sponsored by Child and Family Services and the Western New York Family Resource Network, will help you help yourself and your family.
- Call Gene Meeks at 842-2750 for more information about the

JOB LOSS RESOURCE PROGRAM.

- Next meeting at ______________________________

Figure 2

JOB SEEKING IN THE CURRENT MARKET
OR
WHERE & HOW TO FIND A JOB

No Charge * Open to everyone

Tuesdays 12:30 - 2:30

Neighborhood House * 179 E. Robie * St. Paul

June 7 WHERE ARE THE JOBS?
by Pat Brennan, Minnesota Job Service
If not in the newspaper ads or the employment agency--where are they?

June 14 TO KEEP GOING AFTER 20 NO'S
by Joanne Parsons, Family Service of Greater Saint Paul
Self Talk--to deal with job rejection and keep going

June 21 JOB READINESS
by Reginald Williams, Wilder Community Assistance Program
How to look for work--an emphasis on the job interview from the employer's view.

June 28 THE ROLLER COASTER SYNDROME
by Jo Kelly, Family Service of Greater Saint Paul
Dealing with the "up and down" feelings during unemployment

- with resource persons from Neighborhood House -

Co-sponsored by Neighborhood House & Family Service of Greater Saint Paul

For more information call Kathy Young at 227-9291 or Joanne Parsons at 222-0311.

Figure 3

UNEMPLOYED BLUES

A SUPPORT GROUP FOR THE UNEMPLOYED

- LOSING HOPE ABOUT THE FUTURE?
- SELF-DOUBTS CREEPING UP ON YOU?
- MOODY AND IRRITABLE WITH YOUR FAMILY?
- PULLING AWAY FROM YOUR FRIENDS?
- FEELING AS THOUGH YOUR WORLD IS FALLING APART?

THESE ARE NOT UNCOMMON RESPONSES TO THE FRUSTRATION OF UNEMPLOYMENT IN A GROUP YOU CAN FIND THE SUPPORT AND UNDERSTANDING OF OTHERS WHO ARE DEALING WITH THE SAME SITUATION AND FEELINGS. YOU WILL LEARN THAT YOU ARE NOT ALONE IN WHAT YOU ARE GOING THROUGH, AND TOGETHER YOU CAN EXPLORE ALTERNATIVE WAYS OF HANDLING YOURSELF DURING THIS CRITICAL PERIOD.

IF YOU SEE YOURSELF IN THIS DESCRIPTION, CONSIDER THE GROUP --

LOOP FAMILY CENTER
UNITED CHARITIES OF CHICAGO
14 EAST JACKSON BLVD. 15TH FLOOR

ORIENTATION SESSION

NOVEMBER 3 9:30 - 11:00 A.M.

GROUP SESSIONS WILL BE OFFERED FREE OF CHARGE

CONTACT FERN GRAF AT **939-1300** IF YOU ARE INTERESTED IN JOINING US.

The size of groups varied from ten to fifty or more persons. In some instances, the groups did not draw many unemployed; sometimes they attracted people who had never been employed. The latter situation apparently tended to occur when groups offered help with job search skills, resume writing, and related matters. In more than one instance, such groups drew mostly women seeking to enter the labor market--an important membership, but not one expected. The leaders of the groups generally had favorable opinions of their outcomes, but, for the most part, no specific follow-up data were obtained on which evaluations could be based.

Direct Job-Related Services

While some of the groups that have been mentioned might be considered to be job-related, we now define the term more narrowly to refer to such services as: job development and job placement; training and retraining programs; career counseling and career goal counseling; work training programs (as in housing rehabilitation); and job resource fairs and related activities that verge on direct employment methods. Overall, agencies in the study did not offer this type of service. One or two referred to staff with special training, but the general use of state and local employment facilities already functioning probably relieved the agencies from having to take up what was an unfamiliar service.

Community Organization and Education

Reporting agencies played a considerable role in these indirect services on behalf of the unemployed. When coalitions were formed, the agencies were often substantially involved, providing coordination, recruiting other organizations for the coalition, and performing similar tasks. They also did much to publicize the plight of the unemployed, the extent of the problem locally, and what the needs were and what the services could and could not do.

4

THE COMMUNITY AND UNEMPLOYMENT

High unemployment can cripple communities as well as individuals and families. The crisis that is caused by the closing of a large factory may require a community-wide mustering of resources to help the jobless and to recover economic health. Whatever the cause of unemployment where they were, the agencies that took part in the survey found themselves uniting with other groups in their communities for providing services, planning, and funding.

COMMUNITY LINKAGES

The survey agencies reported making extensive use of many other agencies in their efforts to help the unemployed. In addition to using job-related services, the agencies needed to refer out for a wide variety of presenting problems, including drug and alcohol abuse, child and spouse abuse, suicidal tendencies, income assistance, housing, and medical care.

Central to efforts to help applicants learn about and reach necessary help was the existence of information and referral services, whether as a separate entity or as one of the services provided by community agencies. Experienced staff were already aware of resources needed to meet problems likely to be presented; they also had a sense of which resources were effective for which clients. Because of personnel turnover, however, both the referring agencies and the resource agencies needed constant updating. Otherwise, valuable time was lost and clients sometimes became discouraged.

Beyond simple information-giving, referral included contacts with resource organizations by staff members of the referring agency. Without such contacts, referrels were believed much less likely to produce worthwhile results.

The many resource agencies in communities can be categorized by certain types of help for the unemployed. Job-related help is available from:

- The local state employment office
- Local and state rehabilitation services
- Training programs
- Vocational counseling and testing
- Displaced homemaker programs
- Specialized employment services (for example, for women or handicapped persons)
- On-the-job training programs

Sources of income maintenance and related services include:

- The local department of social service (welfare or human resources)
- Religious organizations
- Family agencies with relief and related services

- Food distribution/meal services centers

- Emergency shelters

Counseling and similar services are provided by:

- Consumer credit counseling services

- Legal aid societies and other legal services

- Mental health agencies and services

- Hospitals

- Alcoholics Anonymous and organizations for other addictions

- Housing services

Although these programs and services do not provide everything needed for comprehensive assistance to the unemployed, they respond to the major needs. Such services obviously should be effective; evaluation of them is a community responsibility. The survey asked the responding agencies to list the three agencies providing the most effective assistance to the unemployed; the variety of answers indicated that level of effectiveness varies considerably. In many communities the basic services were rated only partly effective at best. Service providers working with the unemployed soon learn which resource organizations do their work well. Advocacy is required to try to upgrade other services.

The question of service effectiveness takes on added meaning when fliers or brochures advising the unemployed where to go for help are widely distributed. It may be a difficult problem to handle, but the welfare of people in distress must take precedence over sparing the feelings of ineffective service organization staff. The advocacy that may be needed to improve services should achieve its goals before services are promoted.

While agency responses regarding special projects for the unemployed did not specifically mention case management, it appears that this is a badly needed function in helping the unemployed. The effective flow and use of resources are much increased with the use of case managers. It may not be feasible to carry out certain aspects of a complete case management system--for example, written agreements among agencies and follow-up conferences--but the basic functions are manageable. A specific staff person acts as case manager for a specific client, helping the client assess the situation and weigh the options for proceeding. There are follow-up contacts to ensure effective service as well as assistance with the referral process. In most communities, the case management function may be assumed primarily by one organization with other agencies providing one or more services to be drawn upon as needed. As an initial step, human service agencies should advocate to make case management an integral part of a helping network for the unemployed.

PLANNING

Although the survey reflected a single point of view--that of agencies reporting only their experiences in their own communities--its findings suggest that in many communities there was little coalitional planning to counter the effects of unemployment. Among the sixty-eight agencies reporting special projects, about 55 percent working coalitions with other organizations. The remaining 45 percent seemed to have worked independently.

While other parts of the survey point to a general spirit of cooperativeness among agencies and other organizations, such cooperation is not the same as planning, coordinating, and integrating services to provide assistance to those who are unemployed.

Broadly speaking, planning would have involved an assessment of needs, services available, and gaps in services. A next step would have been to determine which agencies were performing needed services, in the event the services had to be expanded. It would have included determining which agencies might institute needed but unavailable services in the community. Further steps would have included assignment of such functions as outreach, community education, training, and consultation.

From materials submitted by some agencies and later discussions with agency representatives, researchers learned that agencies tended to go through their own planning process, usually involving some of the suggested planning considerations. For the most part, the survey response gives the impression of agencies rallying to a pressing need rather than putting into effect existing plans or drawing on a reservoir of community planning information.

Planning also requires some form of ongoing monitoring of the unemployment problem, with assessments of various needs and services as they emerge and with continuing contacts with employers, unions, and other organizations that are directly involved.

Such continual planning functions should also include attention to funding. While competition for scarce funding dollars for social services will certainly continue, each community needs to make the effort to assure rational utilization of funds according to a plan for services. In some communities represented in the survey, strong efforts were made in this direction. In Detroit, for example, funding of agencies was directed by an overall plan of attack on unemployment problems.

The survey indicated that, in many communities, the basis for ongoing planning and cooperation exists in the form of interagency linkages. The anticipated problems of territorial competition and other reasons for resistance do not seem pervasive, although they were found in a few communities. Advocacy efforts are needed in such places.

Ideally, some type of centralized interagency group is indicated, under the auspices of an organization such as the United Way. Without ongoing attention, it seems likely that a community will be unprepared for an employment crisis, or even for the "normal" unemployment that is likely to remain fairly high.

FUNDING SOURCES

Survey findings showed that funds for special projects came from a variety of sources. Some projects were funded primarily from a single source; some received smaller amounts from several sources; and some were funded by the agency out of its operating budget, usually through allocation of existing staff time to the project.

The most frequent funding source was the local United Way, which often responded to the emergent needs of the unemployed. Other sources included:

- Religious organizations (churches and temples, singly or through denominational structures; affiliated lay groups and affiliated religous organizations)

- Government (local government units, including departments of social services; special grants from city government; assistance in such concrete matters as transportation)

- Local foundations

- Local donors (contributions from agency board members and others)

- Unions (generally, available funds were directed toward their members, but some unions contributed in various ways toward a more general effort)

The list is not exclusive; agencies should be creative in developing other funding sources, establishing and maintaining connections that can be used in a time of economic crisis.

For example, advocacy can be directed toward urging state governments to develop plans for future recessions, with specific types of funding to be made available locally and by contract. Many state governments now are tending to provide funding or services that were formerly handled through federal sources. Similar efforts also can be directed to city governments, but considerable preparation is needed to bring together departments and other governmental subdivisions to fashion joint plans for action.

Working through or developing ecumenical councils or coalitions provides a way of connecting with many religious groups, thus involving many more people in funding. Ecumenical sponsorship also helps to persuade other sources of funds, such as businesses, that the total effort is worthy.

The agencies in the survey reported that corporations provided little or no help in special project funding. To some extent, corporate funding may have been involved in United Way special help. For the future, planning to finance help for victims of unemployment should include strategies for approaching corporations.

Another approach to large corporations would be to urge them to include a provision in employee assistance programs for help in the event of layoffs or plant closings. Group meetings of those being terminated could help them prepare for unemployment; the participation of unions and other agencies at the same time would facilitate the process. Some individuals would need counseling, which, in some instances, would go beyond a consideration of their unemployment into family matters. This approach might also appeal to management as good public relations at a critical time, and even pave the way for further contributions from corporations.

An avenue to businesses, particularly small businesses, can be found in service clubs such as the Rotary club or the Lions club, which often give small grants. In addition, talks by agency representatives to such groups may elicit "in-kind" assistance from business people, particularly in concrete services such as the maintenance of houses.

Other local groups such as civic associations, neighborhood associations, and ethnic organizations could be approached. Such organizations have little or no money to give, but they or individual members may provide in-kind help. They can also be brought into support networks, to help with such work as job searching, and with locating housing, etc.

While the funding of a special project may be accomplished with the help of only one or two sources, it seldom happens that way. Instead, agencies try to locate many sources of small grants and contributions. Doing so, they build a broader community awareness by having more groups involved. Such fund raising, however, is very time consuming, and agencies may well hesitate to allocate so much staff time to it. One solution is to enlist more volunteer help, possibly linking the fund raising to volunteers already engaged in advocacy or other work for the agency.

Clearly, communities that have ongoing mechanisms for cooperative efforts will be in a much better position to start fund raising; community data and support will be at hand already and lengthy delay and confusion may be avoided. Applications for funding can be quickly drawn up; community groups and councils that can help already exist. Funding sources are impressed that preparations have been made and that the best use of money, staff, and volunteers has been generally agreed upon. The results of the survey, together with data from the literature, provide sound guidance for such advanced planning.

5

MODEL PROGRAMS

Responses to the survey included descriptions of special projects that were undertaken to help the unemployed and their families. The projects included the organizing of groups and the provision of concrete, clinical, and combined services. A few of the descriptions are summarized here to illustrate the concept of special projects. They are models for projects in the sense that they show in concise detail how such projects functioned. The few examples chosen represent several others; a number of agencies conducted similar projects and, for the most part, were satisfied with the results.

GROUPS FOR THE UNEMPLOYED

The survey agencies reported that they had organized a variety of groups that had a common objective: helping the participants obtain reemployment. The groups were quite different in structure; some were self-help groups, and others involved agency staff members in different numbers and levels of responsibility. The topics of group meetings covered such matters as resume writing, job search skills, job readiness, job finders networks, stress management, and coping skills. A typical group would meet for six sessions.

New Jersey: In Morristown, Family Service of Morris County developed and conducted a special project for the unemployed that grew out of a displaced homemaker program. It was directed to single parents living in the community--those who had been divorced, separated, or widowed. Most of the participants had had little experience working for a salary but they all needed employment. Typically, a group member was a thirty-five-year-old divorced white woman from the lower income level of the middle class; she had gone to high school, lacked self-esteem, and was angry over her situation. The agency raised funds from contributions, the United Way, and federal grants, using the money to hire full-time staff members to lead the group. It built attendance at meetings by promotion in the media, personal visits to possible participants, speaking engagements, open houses, and notices enclosed with welfare checks. One-day job readiness workshops were conducted at a variety of times and places for six weeks. Topics included resume writing, job applications and interviews, dressing for interviews, and handling job stress. Group leaders also referred participants to training opportunities and to specialized job services. In retrospect, one can observe that the group was aimed at a part of society that is at great risk of economic deprivation. Such people tend to respond when they learn that help is available and to accept agency services. Because they lack much work experience, they need a group whose leaders can contribute substantial information about finding jobs.

<u>Washington</u>: Family Services of King County in Seattle conducted a project for college-educated people who had never had to hunt for a job but who were newly unemployed. Using the media and promotional literature, the agency offered a three-hour seminar on "Coping with Unemployment: Energizing Yourself for the Job Search." Such seminars were designed to help participants develop coping skills and strategies, identify transferable skills, and build personal contacts. The project was part of a

broad coalition effort supported by other agencies and by religious groups and, to some extent, the labor council; most of the costs, however, were paid by the family agency. Comparing this activity with the preceding one, the difference in format should be noted, as should be the fact that the Seattle project operated as part of a coalition effort. The different format and range of services were tailored for a different group of people and in relation to other community activities. The project did not cost as much as the one in New Jersey.

Kentucky: Family and Children's Agency of Louisville undertook a program with a more general purpose. Staff members visited union halls, churches, and other community sites to make presentations to workers who were about to be laid off from large factories. Their purpose was to urge their listeners to seek help promptly for personal or family problems related to unemployment.

Oklahoma: People indirectly troubled because of increased unemployment were the objectives of an effort undertaken by Family and Children's Service of Tulsa. The agency conducted a year-long stress management program for employees at the state employment office, who were working under extreme pressure.

These educational programs and others like them that were reported in the survey were customarily carried on by social workers, usually staff members of the agencies involved. Occasionally the agencies recruited other helpers because of their special expertise.

In summary, the survey results indicated that educational groups are helpful to the unemployed for a number of reasons. Conducting groups is an activity with which the reporting agencies were familiar, and sponsorship does not involve large expenditures of money unless the program is extensive.

CONCRETE SERVICES

The needs that result from a high level of unemployment in a community are likely to require community groups to develop service programs with concrete goals. The programs reported by three agencies in response to the survey provide examples of such activities.

California: Family Service of Los Angeles, as part of a coalition of social service agencies and other organizations, received funding to provide financial assistance to eligible applicants. The money was used to give food vouchers and money for rent or emergency shelter.

Pennsylvania: Family and Community Service of Delaware County, whose main office is in Media, offered emergency food assistance for jobless people who were temporarily out of money. This, too, was part of a broad, coalition effort. The program was carried on at a number of sites; the funding came from a variety of sources. Social workers from the agency were stationed at food distribution centers to provide applicants with information and referral help if it was needed.

Iowa: Financial counseling designed to meet the problems of the unemployed was developed by the Family Service Agency of Cedar Rapids. Primary emphases were on money management, budgeting, and effective shopping habits. This program was also a coalition effort and was carried on by volunteers.

A number of survey agencies providing such services indicated that they should be made available on a permanent basis, thus recognizing that a relatively high level of unemployment is ongoing and that government assistance may fall short.

CLINICAL SERVICES

The survey report showed a need for clinical services to help with problems engendered or exacerbated by unemployment. It identified a number of agencies that set up special projects in which casework staff worked with people with such problems.

Family Service of Racine, Wisconsin, for example, obtained a special United Way grant to provide twenty hours a week of counseling to the unemployed who applied for help with stress-related individual and family problems. Referrals to the agency came through publicity and from a labor representative at the United Way. In the agency's judgment, the program was effective in helping the jobless cope with stresses; it was not oriented to job-related service.

Other agencies represented in the survey offered clinical services as part of broader programs whose principal emphases were on job finding, information and referral, and other activities directly related to working. Most agencies followed a pattern of providing clinical help to the unemployed as part of regular counseling services. Such a pattern may be the most feasible course for an agency, but better service is likely to result if counseling help is planned as something separate from other services.

COMBINED SERVICES

Survey agencies that were situated in large urban areas tended to offer a range of services to the unemployed, usually as part of a coalition or in collaboration with unions. Such combined efforts were conceived as community projects; the agency's role might change from time to time, dpending on such factors as funding and needs. Working together brought about closer relationships among the participating organizations, and there was a lessening of competitive spirit over services and areas of work.

The experiences of Oakland Family Services of Pontiac, Michigan, were representative of other agencies. It was one of seven family agencies in the area that were linked in a broad coalition supported United Way funding. The area suffered a high level of chronic unemployment. Seeking to be of help, agencies developed extensive referral networks. The Oakland agency's contribution to the combined effort included individual and group counseling, career exploration and planning, and job search networking. A networking form was used to help clients develop contacts systematically; it required a client to list family members, former colleagues at work, acquaintances from high school, congregation, hobby group, community activities, and professional circles.

In summary, reviewing the results of the survey --in particular the different services performed by the survey agencies--points to the conclusion that assisting the unemployed is a feasible activity for most agencies. The varied nature of aid to the jobless--the range of possible services, the different funding sources, the several ways of structuring community involvement--indicate that there are many paths that an agency can follow in finding its particular place and role.

Studying the results also reveals the essential role of planning, for it is clear that many of the projects were too slow in getting under way and that many community efforts were inadequate to the tasks that faced them.

6

STAFF AND VOLUNTEERS

For the most part, agencies responding to the survey reported that they used their regular staff members in providing services to the unemployed. The amount of service was not large, however; the agencies noted that one of their primary needs in working with the unemployed was for more staff. Survey results showed that only six agencies had full-time staff working exclusively with the jobless, and only nine agencies had staff members who worked half-time or more on such assignments. A scattering of agencies said staff worked less than half-time on the problem.

When agencies were engaged in a special project related to unemployment, they used their regular staff for the work. Generally, when such a project was financed by special funding, the agencies were able to allocate existing staff to the project exclusively or they hired staff for that purpose.

Although most of the agency staffs, whether or not working exclusively with the unemployed, appear to have had master's degrees in social work, there were also workers with BSW degrees or degrees in related fields.

One of the interesting aspects revealed by the survey was the extent to which agencies used outside resource people and the variety of expertise represented by such people. Agencies sought help from persons knowledgeable in specialized fields related to employment. Some were experts in resume writing, job clubs and networks, career counseling, vocational counseling, labor practices, and personnel matters. Others specialized in financial matters, including counseling, budgeting, and legal help. Some had mastered the fields of welfare, entitlements, and social policy. For the most part, such people were recruited by agencies engaged in special projects. Some agencies used them also in the preparation of materials, including guides in such areas as job search skills and career counseling, and in the publishing of directories.

While agencies participated in interagency meetings--including training sessions--in some communities, survey responses indicated that they proceeded on their own in the area of training and consultation. It would seem that, with planning, much more could be done in making training and consultation available throughout a community, bringing agencies together more closely in a coherent system of services for the unemployed. Such training might then be more easily available to more agency staff members, strengthening their efforts to help the unemployed in their caseloads, either separately or concurrently with a special project.

USE OF VOLUNTEERS

Although volunteers should not be used to take the place of staff members, they can augment the work of staff in various ways. In the survey, most agencies did not indicate that they used volunteers to assist in carrying out services. There were exceptions; one agency, for example, found that volunteers were a significant help in doing information and referral work.

Customarily, agencies tend to refrain from utilizing volunteers in direct service because doing so involves sensitive issues that may be difficult to handle. First, probably, is that of role definition, which includes the corollary question of displacing staff with volunteers. A second important issue is couched often in either-or terms, so that it appears that a choice must be made between all staff or all volunteers in a given type of service. Other questions relate to difficulties in recruiting and screening, training and supervising, and fitting the volunteers into the agency staff structure without undue friction.

Consideration of the types of services--other than those that are clinical and educational--that agencies might offer to the unemployed shows that several concrete services can be carried out in part by volunteers who are suitably trained and supervised. One such example has already been cited, that of information and referral. Volunteers have also been successful in budgeting and financial counseling as well as financial assistance. These areas, according to the survey, were those in which the unemployed most needed help, apart from direct job-related services.

Volunteers for these and similar tasks can be obtained with sufficient investment of forethought and effort. Recruiting them is only the first step. Orientation, training, and job placement are crucial in working with volunteers if they are to be retained and if they are to put effort and commitment in their work.

An agency should have little trouble in maintaining an ample body of volunteers. Sometimes the number available may fluctuate because of conditions in a community--people who might ordinarily be available are involved in seasonal work or are away on holidays--but these variables can be considered in planning. In addition, there are sources other than the usual community pool of helpers. Agencies may be able to utilize undergraduate or graduate social work students who are looking for field work placements. People who are unemployed may be interested in volunteering because of a special interest in helping others or because they see volunteer service as on-the-job training that might qualify them for a possible new career.

Students, as part of their field work, may undertake the supervision of volunteers. While it is true that core staffing is essential to maintain such volunteer work, many concrete services can be clearly defined and allotted to various levels of personnel, including volunteers.

An early prototype for the use of volunteers in such services was the citizens' advice bureaus that were started in England during World War II and that continued afterward because of their outstanding usefulness. The bureaus were staffed by volunteers under the supervision of paid professionals.

An Agency's Experience

Volunteers serving in one capacity have the potential for developing new skills. The agency that responded to the survey with a report on using volunteers for information and referral indicated that there were additional developments. From information and referral work, for which they were trained and supervised by staff, the volunteers' involvement was extended to include other functions as the needs arose. When guiding people to services and entitlements did not meet all their needs, volunteers were trained in case advocacy to help clients obtain the services and entitlements. Financial assistance, primarily in very small amounts, became essential; clients needing a dollar or two immediately to help them get to an employment interview or to a new job could not be turned away. Small grants were sometimes necessary for food or other expenses to tide a family over when a breakdown in government procedures caused a crisis.

In short, it became evident that, if the service was to function effectively as a crisis center for the unemployed and others in special need, it had to be able to help with urgent problems on the spot. Furthermore, it had to be able to press for other solutions through negotiation, cooperation, and advocacy. As the center developed in these ways, working there became a more meaningful activity for volunteers, and their motivation increased. Their training had to be more comprehensive, but they gained a sense of competence from it. They felt that they were something more than human computers spouting out answers to simple questions.

The service was primarily a storefront operation, with staff and volunteers working closely together. The staff provided much of the training, supervised on an "as needed" basis for the most part, and became involved only in the most difficult cases, sometimes with volunteers, sometimes without. The professional workers also were responsible for understanding the broader manifestations of client situations and behaviors and for direct referral to clinical or other services.

Job Definition and Training

Job definition and training are critical to maintaining the motivation and efforts of volunteers. Since volunteers work only a short segment of hours each week, multiple functions that a staff member might perform may have to be distributed into several jobs for volunteers. Generally, such particularized assignments are most suitable when they accomodate a volunteer's needs in terms of amount of time and frequency of service--once a week or once a month, for example. Once the functions are determined and the volunteer's abilities are assessed, training can be provided.

There are general guidelines that can be followed in job definition. They relate to the functions that are part of every job an agency undertakes:

Planning involves clarification of the problem or problems that would be addressed by the proposed service; surveying what is being done and has been done locally; gathering general information on the subject; initiating a plan for further steps.

Organizing requires outlining the steps in the work and determining the staff members, volunteers, and other people and agencies needed; arranging for coalitions and networks if they are relevant.

Training is preparing agency staff and volunteers, as well as other people who are involved, for the activities.

Direction and coordination of the people and agencies taking part in the activity.

Arranging has to do with setting up the details of meetings and training sessions, with the preparation and production of materials, with providing support services to staff and volunteers who are engaged in the activity.

Action, which means carrying out the various activities that the job comprises.

There are five elements in training:

Program, which has to do with the nature of the service and its place in the agency.

Concerns of the service--that is, the problems that the service is to respond to. This element includes the difficulties that are likely to obstruct the service. It also covers related community problems and community groups.

Experiential training involves field visits to relevant sites, contacts with client, consumer, and other groups. It also incudes observing the work of people who are providing the service.

Sensitivity training is intended to help trainees recognize their own feelings about the group of people with whom they will be dealing and to develop their understanding of the life situations and feelings and attitudes of such groups.

Knowledge, which refers to the trainees' knowledge base, which usually needs to be supplemented by on-going training.

How these elements of job definition and training may combine in an actual situation can be illustrated by a hypothetical example. In this case, an agency is contemplating using volunteers to launch and conduct an information and referral service for unemployed people in its community. Using the elements of job definition to analyze the situation, the agency could determine that volunteers could possibly be utilized at several stages. For instance, members of the agency's board of directors, as well as other volunteers, could take part in the initial planning, and some of the same people might continue to be involved in the organizing phase. Training and direction and coordination are functions that most likely would be done by paid staff members. The arranging and action phases, however, offer opportunities for volunteers. Generally, initial and on-going training programs for volunteers are highly desirable in every phase of activity. As an example, planning is enhanced and made more relevant if the volunteers are given experiential and sensitivity training. Training is obviously essential for actual service functions.

There would be value in involving unemployed persons as volunteers in an information and referral service. Such involvement would be made feasible by careful job descriptions and brief, concentrated training programs. Using unemployed people in this way brings them the benefits of helping themselves. Agencies in the survey reported such benefits in the mutual-aid job-search groups that they sponsored.

7

ADVOCACY

The agencies responding to the survey reported that only 5 percent or less of their time and budgets were invested in advocacy. Several agencies said they had no specific advocacy programs; a few allocated much more than 5 percent of their resources to the activity. The survey results indicate little in regard to the need for advocacy in dealing with unemployment problems--either at the case level (helping an individual) or the cause level (trying to bring about institutional change). There are hints that agency staff turned to people outside the agency for help in dealing with problems in such areas as welfare and entitlements; the implication is that the clients involved in these matters needed agency staff to advocate for them.

The reports in the survey on special projects for the unemployed showed no emphasis on advocacy, and, as previously noted, the fairly consistent high ratings of cooperation among community agencies seemed to indicate that perhaps advocacy was not sorely needed.

As a general observation aside from survey results, it can be said that, in most agencies with advocacy programs, the advocating is aimed at a variety of important issues. The advocacy staff is fully committed. Some of the issues may relate to the specific topic of unemployment, but staff time is too limited to allow much effort to be directed to that topic or any other single problem.

Helping people meet the problems of unemployment in the future may require greater use of advocacy. To assess its potential for that purpose, it is helpful to consider these comments:

"...Advocacy goals include not only improvement of existing public voluntary services and their delivery, but also provision of new or changed forms of social utilities..."[1]

Advocacy has been described as "opposition to negative impacts of social institutions and systems on people, individually and in groups (including neighborhoods, communities, ethnic and other groups)...promotion of measures to support and enhance human life individually and generally."[2]

Advocacy can be distinguished from other types of efforts at change by its characteristic "potentially adversarial stance on issues."[3] In an agency, advocacy tends to move from "case to cause," based on the agency's experience with the problems of the people it serves.

From these perspectives, it is possible to see that advocacy can be important in helping the unemployed. For example, one highly important function is to determine what services may be needed for the unemployed but do not exist; the aim would be to campaign for the development of these services. Awareness of such needs could arise from knowledge of individuals requiring the services or from already existing knowledge based on planning. The advocacy might be aimed at funding organizations that could support needed services or at existing agencies, such as government offices, which should provide the services. Advocacy activities in this case could include public education, development of citizen and consumer groups, and pressure on government.

Case advocacy would be highly important apart from such specific problems as getting assistance from organizations that resist providing it. Bureaucracies often need pressure because of the glut of documents in government offices, the misunderstandings and misinterpretations of laws and regulations that occur, and countless other human and procedural imperfections. Agency advocate staff must always be alert and knowledgeable about services and benefits, so that they can detect such problems. Otherwise, there is a tendency to accept what has happened as being correct. Case advocacy is an integral part of rendering concrete services to clients. Possible ways of helping the unemployed and their families include:[4]

<u>Food and clothing</u>
Emergency food and clothing provisions
Clothing provision--free or subsidized, uniform and work supplies
<u>Housing</u>
Shelter for homeless, transients, etc.
Housing counseling, information, location assistance
Rehabilitation, repair, renovation, restoration, etc.
Mortgage and loan assistance
Provision of furniture, supplies, tools, etc.
<u>Financial resources</u>
Emergency financial assistance
Financial counseling
AFDC
General financial assistance
Food stamps
Social Security
Supplemental Security Income
Unemployment insurance
Veterans' benefits
Workmen's compensation
Other disability, retirement, death benefits

Health insurance--including Medicare, Medicaid

Employment

Counseling, testing

Job development

Training--on the job, public service, etc.

Job placement

Enforcement of equal opportunity, affirmative action, minimum wage, etc.

Health

Counseling, information

Emergency medical care

Testing, diagnostic evaluation

General medical care--outpatient

Medical care--inpatient

Dental care

Provision of medication, medical supplies and equipment

Social-emotional development, adjustment

Emergency services--drug, alcohol, mental health, etc.

Personal and family counseling

Diagnostic and evaluative services

Self-help groups

Protection from abuse, neglect, exploitation

Education, information service

Protective services--adults, children

Shelter

Investigation services--adults, children

Day care

After-school care

Education and information

Day care centers

Family day care

Community organization and information

Information dissemination and referral

Information and referral service

Community education and information (on alcohol, consumer affairs, drugs, environmental problems, mental health, health, etc.)

Advocacy (generally and in relation to various subjects--child care, education, consumers, housing,

legal issues, etc.)
Voluntary fund raising
Community and human relations
Civil rights
Community planning
Economic development (small business, industry, tourism, etc.)
Occupational and professional groups
Service planning
Volunteers (recruitment, placement, training, types of uses, etc.)

Transportation

Car pool information
Transportation information
Public transit

WHERE ADVOCACY IS NEEDED

While many agencies cannot by themselves mount advocacy campaigns on state and national levels, they need to know what is happening at those levels and to consider the implications for their communities. To illustrate the point, retraining programs might be available in a state in only one or two localities even though they are needed in other places as well. Advocating for wider distribution of the programs should be directed at the state government. A group of similar agencies in the state can be linked for such a purpose. There may be other organizations in the region--some with entree to the state government--that have the same interests and that would welcome the opportunity to participate in the advocacy effort.

Agencies in cities and other communities can contribute to advocacy efforts that are national in scope. They can provide documentation--case material, studies, and surveys--from their activities that will support national organizations advocating on their behalf. They can participate in regional and national conferences and other activities that publicize programs that they support--help for the unemployed, for example.

Advocacy at any level should be ongoing to be most effective; it is not an activity that will realize its full potential if it is organized quickly to respond to an emergency situation. In addition, advocacy efforts need stability in financial resources. One conclusion drawn from the results of the survey was that money in support of advocacy seems to be most available if the concerns and needs of a community are carefully identified and addressed.

REFERENCES

1. Ellen Manser, ed., Family Advocacy: A Manual for Action (New York: Family Service Association of America, 1973).
2. Robert Sunley, Advocating Today: A Human Service Practitioner's Handbook (New York: Family Service America, 1983), p. 9.
3. Ibid., p. 10.
4. Adapted from Sunley, Advocating Today, pp. 60-65.

8

PREVENTION: NOW AND THE FUTURE

Preventing unemployment is a utopian goal, but preventing lives from being damaged or destroyed because of joblessness is a practical objective for a society and for its human service agencies.

The survey showed that agencies, for example, can undertake interventions to help people deal with the impact of layoffs, plant shutdowns, and sudden recessions. Such efforts may include providing individual and group counseling to workers in a plant where a mass layoff is planned, of where notices have already gone out. A few agencies have been involved in this type of prevention, usually in conjunction with a labor union. The impact of unemployment can be mitigated to some extent by informing workers about the approach of a crisis, for example, or the facts of job search or the use of existing networks of help. People about to lose their jobs can prepare for it by husbanding their resources, taking time to think through what they can do, and making contacts with helping organizations.

This type of prevention by agencies often will function best if carried out with unions. Such arrangements can exist on an ongoing basis, not waiting for a crisis. United Ways can take the lead in this or provide the support and encouragement required. Cooperative involvement of large companies also should be part of this planning and often can be approached through the United Way.

The experiences of the agencies covered in the survey also point to the need for more advocacy that has a preventive purpose. For example, an agency might work with unions and other groups to persuade major employers in a community to institute a plan to lessen unemployment during a recession by adjusting work force schedules. Workers sometimes can be kept on the job if hours of work are shortened, shifts are cut, and short furloughs are given. These measures have been used effectively in some situations. Such an agreement can require much time and effort before it is finally reached, but the program to achieve it has value in itself because it represents a means of engaging employers in discussion of the measures if the need arises.

Yet another focus of advocacy might be to propose that employers give advance notification of closings or shutdowns. Such a policy has been followed in European countries--indeed, it is a legal requirement in some countries. Despite employers' fears, it seems to help workers and communities.

The financial support system for the unemployed in this country is seriously inadequate, particularly for those who are jobless for a long time--who have exhausted unemployment insurance benefits--and those who have few resources even for short-term unemployment--for example, the single-parent families and minority families in lower income levels. Being aware of their vulnerabilities should persuade us of the need to assist them at the national and state levels. Agencies can join in such assistance efforts, although they usually are able to contribute little. Locally, however, preventive activities can be initiated, guided by considerations of groups likely to be most in need, how they can be quickly reached, and how resources can be best used.

A number of the agencies responding to the survey pointed out this important aspect of prevention: Those most needing help often do not know what to do and are not reached quickly. "They wait too long," is a common comment. Thus one preventative measure that can be taken in a community is to reduce that "waiting," which in turn reduces the impact of unemployment.

In past recessions, the impact of unemployment was uneven. Its effect differed from one individual and family to the next, depending not only on resources and quickly finding another job, but also on such factors as a neighborhood or extended family network which provided emotional support, part-time employment, help with debt, and aid in job-hunting for family members who hadn't worked before. But not everyone has such networks and, with long-term unemployment, even support networks tend to pull back and give up. It seems likely that areas with populations that are more mobile than average and that have fewer community roots will suffer more acutely.

While there are no specific guidelines for creating the equivalents of such natural networks, a study of how a community responded to the last recession may reveal to what extent and in what ways such networks operated. This, in turn, may suggest how agencies can find substitutes which can be in place before another unemployment crisis occurs.

THE FUTURE

The recession of 1981-82 left its mark on many people. "Bad times" lingered for many months and in some parts of the nation there has been only sporadic improvement. Today, communities that are largely dependent on one large factory or industry are still at risk. In urban areas, low-income people--especially minorities and single-parent families--

continue to experience a constant, fairly high rate of unemployment. When and where a new recession will strike is a matter of conjecture, but experience indicates that it may not be far off.

The many kinds of vulnerability to economic crisis and the uncertainty about the places that may be hurt next by declines in the job market mean that agencies can look to no single prescription to help the unemployed. In general, however, two courses of action can be taken. The first is to respond to present unemployment problems, serving jobless workers and their families where they exist, according to their needs and the resources available to the agencies. The second is to prepare now to meet the needs of the unemployed when a new recession occurs. Most agencies will have one of these roles if not both.

Coping with an ongoing high unemployment situation in a community is perhaps more difficult than responding to a crisis. The initial appeal for help loses its persuasiveness, funding sources are less impressed or lose heart, and unemployment becomes a chronic condition with aggravated problems. The agency finds difficulty in continuing its services. In answers to the survey, agencies reported that they were frequently frustrated in getting new funds to continue services after the initial funding, stimulated by a crisis, had been depleted.

Responses to the survey and subsequent discussion of them indicated that reporting agencies found a variety of ways to respond to crisis situations, either alone or in conjunction with other organizations. Generally, the major questions in confronting a crisis are:

- What is being done for the unemployed? By which organizations?

- What is not being done, or what services should be increased?

- What resources does the agency have? Can it rearrange its priorities and provide the internal supports needed--such as technical assistance? Can new funding be found?

- Can coalitions be built or expanded? Can planning and monitoring be handled this way?

- Is there one agency that is able to take the initiative or to help initiate preventive efforts, public education, and advocacy?

The severe impact of unemployment on many families points to the need for comprehensive responses ranging from coalitions and networks to integrated systems of help. The integrated system represents an ideal concept, a locality or center where a wide range of services is provided. In such a center, the unemployed are more quickly directed to needed services, and concurrent use of services is more likely and more feasible. Most or all of the services described in earlier chapters would be available within the center. Definite service agreements would involve services provided at and by other organizations. The comprehensive community mental health center represents a parallel organization: it is constituted of certain essential elements under a common direction. The concept of a center for the unemployed has been approximated in some urban areas where several organizations have worked together; full realization of the concept, however, needs demonstration to test its methods.

One way to develop support for the establishment of such a center might be by initiating studies that would show the long term effects of unemployment. Support also might be engendered if data were collected on single-parent families, their vulnerability to unemployment, and the resources needed to help them.

The concept has some similarities to the role of the welfare system in helping the unemployed. Despite its shortcomings, the welfare system acts as a back-up in assisting the jobless. Many recipients remain on welfare only a fairly short time; the system also helps the long-term unemployed and those who are without unemployment benefits.[1]

The data that would come from such studies of unemployment and the findings of the FSA-NAF survey would provide human service agencies with the information necessary to plan centers to serve the unemployed.

REFERENCE

1. Greg J. Duncan et al., Years of Poverty, Years of Plenty: The Changing Economic Fortunes of American Workers and Families (Ann Arbor, MI: Institute for Sociological Research, 1984).

APPENDIX 1

SERVING THE UNEMPLOYED*

BY ESTHER KRYSTAL, MARSHA MORAN-SACKETT, SYLVIA V. THOMPSON, AND LUCILE CANTONI

Unemployment in the United States is unusually high. The United States Bureau of Labor reports that the national unemployment rate was 10.4 percent at the end of October 1982. The percentage would have been higher if the number of discouraged workers (those who have not looked for work in over four weeks) and the number of underemployed workers had been included. The 10.4 percent translated to 11.6 million people out of work.[1]

Certain populations had higher unemployment rates than others: women maintaining families had a rate of 11.2 percent, while married men "with spouse present" had a rate of 7.6 percent. Unemployment among blacks was 20.2 percent and among Hispanics, 15.2 percent. The teenage (sixteen years to nineteen years) unemployment rate was 24 percent. Black teenagers had an unemployment rate of 46.7 percent, white teenagers, 21.7 percent.

---

*From Social Casework: The Journal of Contemporary Social Work 7 (February 1983): 67-75.

The Midwest, Michigan in particular, is noted for the highest rate of unemployment (Michigan's was 16.1 percent in October 1982). However, the entire country feels the effects of auto and construction industries' problems. According to the Michigan Employment Security Commission, the Detroit Metropolitan area had an unemployment rate of 15.2 percent in September 1982. There has been news of more company closings since then, as well as other layoffs, and so it is anticipated that this area's rate will continue to increase.[2]

Counselors must attend to their own mental health in order to be available to their unemployed clients. They need supervisors who can "hear" their upset and help them regain perspective. They need support from colleagues. They need to share with each other ways they have been able to serve unemployed clients effectively. Above all, they need to take care of themselves by maintaining a balance of healthy diversions in order to feel relaxed and reduce anxiety. They need to nourish themselves so that they have sufficient energy to work effectively. Burnout is not from too much work; it is from the negative feelings that are attached to the work. If therapists feel ineffective, inadequate, and tired, burnout will occur more quickly.

AN OPPORTUNITY FOR GROWTH

Unemployed people have tangible needs which must be met. Many unemployed people need to learn how to find necessary resources to maintain food and shelter. Of almost equal importance, unemployed people and their families often need help to survive the social and emotional crises which result from unemployment.

Unemployed clients are likely to present physical symptoms including chest pains, shortness of breath, headaches, dizziness, dry mouth, and eczema. They may feel weak, always tired, unable to sleep. They may suffer a loss of self-esteem. Their emotional state may interfere with effective job seeking. Unemployment becomes a family crisis. Marital problems may appear. The children may present symptoms of stress.

Losing a job is experienced by an individual as a loss of a part of the self. The unemployed individual needs to recognize the validity of the pain associated with this loss. He or she must grieve the loss of the job before being able to go on with his or her life.

People may need help to maintain their physical and emotional health during unemployment. Unemployment, like any life crisis, can provide individuals, families, and communities with an opportunity for growth. Old patterns may be reviewed and better patterns for living may be developed.

Unemployed people are confronted by various survival problems. First, they must get food and maintain shelter. Unemployment compensation and public welfare are established to help take care of these needs. Although the post-World War II United States has assumed that there is an economic net that catches peole in times of economic crisis, the net is not entirely effective. When the economic downturn worsened in the Detroit area, the whole community needed to organize to assure that unemployed people had access to resurces to care for their physical needs.

Unemployment is not only a financial crisis, it is also an emotional and social crisis. This fact became apparent in the hard hit Detroit area, where depression, suicidal fears, family violence, and other family breakdowns have increased.

FAMILY SERVICE PROJECTS TO SERVE THE UNEMPLOYED

Family Service of Detroit and Wayne County, with the cooperation and support of six other family service agencies in the tri-county area, developed a program for the unemployed. This program was called Operation FAST (Families Acquiring Survival Tools). It was funded for one year by a special grant from the United Community Services of Metropolitan Detroit. Operation FAST, started in August 1980, was a three-level program.

The first level of Operation FAST was coordination. Representatives from each of the auto companies and each of the major service providers were brought together on an advisory board. The advisory board administered Operation FAST. Second, but equally important, the advisory board provided its members an opportunity to share informally with each other how their respective organizations were adapting to the crisis.

The second level of Operation FAST promoted community awareness of services available to help individuals and families survive. Three community forums were held throughout the metropolitan area. Up to 120 organizations and agencies--for example, utility companies, banks, Ys, public assistance--manned booths. Representatives of these organizations were available to talk to unemployed people about how to avoid losing a home or having utilities cut off, where to find inexpensive recreation, and how to apply for assistance.

The third level of Operation FAST addressed the social and emotional needs of the unemployed. At the forums and through news media programs, public education was provided on the social and emotional effects of unemployment. Support groups were organized to provide direct services to attend to such needs.

When funding for Operation FAST ended in 1981, the seven family service agencies' program for the unemployed shifted to focus on the third level--the social and emotional survival of the unemployed. People who are unemployed, those who are underemployed, and those who anticipate losing their jobs are counseled together with members of their families through a project called Special Outreach to the Unemployed.

The project has gathered data on 964 familes[3] served during its first six months; 42 percent of the people are self-referred, 58 percent are referred by a variety of other community resources. In 40 percent of cases, the unemployed wage earner is the husband of a husband-wife family; 18 percent involve single parents. The other 42 percent are other family members and single persons. Of the 964 unemployed people, 43 percent had actually been laid off, 10 percent were fired, and 12 percent had quit their jobs. The remaining 35 percent lost their jobs for a variety of other reasons. Clients had been unemployed an average of 30.1 weeks when they sought services.

Only 18.9 percent of the people requesting service were formerly employed in the auto industry. Forty-six percent of the clients served had been employed in unskilled or semi-skilled occupations, 27 percent were unskilled, and 19 percent were semiskilled.

These figures indicate that nearly half of the people who apply for service do not have financial resources or marketable skills. Many of the clients' initial requests are for help to maintain utilities, to get emergency food, and to obtain needed clothing. However, other people come into the office because of concerns related to marital problems, problems with parent-child relationships, and depression. The majority of people express feelings of helplessness about their situation, in the face of what appears an unending economic erosion.

A typical client is a middle-aged male presenting a variety of physical symptoms. During the interview, the unemployed person may casually remark that he is going bankrupt and is unable to pay his bills. In the past he lived "the good life," took vacations, owned two cars, and lived in a good neighborhood. The main presenting problem is his obvious depression. This depression makes him feel weak, tired all the time, and unable to sleep well. This person is unable to perform the home chores that he previously did when he was employed. Most of his time is spent eating, reading the paper, and watching television. He feels helpless, is frightened of the future, and lacks hope of finding a job. He mentions that he has applied for many jobs without success. He has begun to withdraw from his former co-workers, friends, and family. The pervading air of depression, if demonstrated to a prospective employer, puts a damper on employment opportunities.

The unemployed person seeking help usually sees himself as a failure in life. He thinks of himself as someone who never measured up to his expectations. He suffers from a loss of self-esteem, shame, and anger because he feels that at this point of his life he should be able to provide an adequate living for his family. Sometimes anger concerning his former boss is verbalized. More often his anger is expressed inwardly through somatic symptoms. There is definitely a loss of self-love.

Although he gives the impression that he is aggressively looking for a job during most of his day, closer examination reveals that his efforts are sporadic, frenzied, or lackluster. He may read the want ads constantly and find nothing. He does not follow through on leads. He may procrastinate about calling about a prospective job until it is too late.

If the man is the head of a family, his unemployment crisis becomes a family crisis. His wife and children may get jobs. There may be no money for family recreational outlets. Marital problems surface. Sexual impotence is common. His wife and children may view his unemployment as a sign of laziness. The homeostasis of the family is altered and each family member is affected by the unemployment. The children may present symptoms of stress. Usually, by the time he comes to the agency, the man's benefits have run out or are about to run out and he feels unable to cope with the situation.

UNEMPLOYMENT AS LOSS OF SELF

Unemployment for most people is experienced as a loss of self and a loss of some aspects of personal functioning.[4] The person is not only confronted by the loss of job, but with loss of those functions which the job provided; food and shelter for one's family, identity, security, competency, independence, and self-esteem. Secondary functional losses relate to the organizing component inherent in work routine and schedule. There is a loss of social and support networks on which the person depends for the expression of feelings and the gratification of emotional needs.

If the unemployed person is the head of a household, his or her loss and grief become the family's loss and grief as well. Family members tend to react to the jobless person's grief with feelings associated with deprivation created by the absence of provisions once supplied by the wage earner. For example, Mr. and Mrs. K, aged thirty and thirty-two years respectively, were a black, middle-class professional couple; she was a retail store manager, he a teacher. Mrs. K called the agency stating that she and her husband wanted marriage counseling. Separated for one month, they had recently reconciled, but "couldn't seem to get past a certain point." Mr. K's recent job resignation and previous layoffs had created much stress in their marriage. The recent separation involved Mr. K's lack of interest in searching for and finding work. As Mrs. K talked, it became clear that she was equating her husband's job instability with her personal sense of security.

Mr. K's loss of job was experienced by Mrs. K as deprivation of love and stimulated her feelings of being uncared for. Mr. K's job loss and attendant grief reaction--depression and anger--were responses to his loss of identity, autonomy, and self-esteem.

MAJOR BEREAVEMENT REACTIONS

Colin Murray Parkes lists seven features[5] that are major elements of many bereavement reactions:

1. Realization of loss
2. Alarm reaction
3. Urge to search for and find lost object
4. Anger and guilt
5. Feelings of internal loss of self or mutilation
6. Identification with symbols of the job
7. Pathological variants of grief

These reactions may be present individually, successively, or collectively. No matter in what constellation they appear, the responses are reactions to a loss. The person is grieving.

The reaction of grief is aimed at resolving and reconciling the loss of the valued object. This activity is termed grieving (grief work), enabling the individual to "call up" the loss as well as to gain some understanding as to its meaning. Grieving is a process which requires time.

Well-meaning friends and loved ones may try to cheer unemployed persons. However, when the unemployed try to express their pain, they may hear, "You shouldn't feel that way." They are often given good advice as to how to look for a job, and when they do not move on the advice, they may be regarded as lazy. Unemployed clients frequently tell a counselor that they cannot discuss their pain with their loved ones for fear of overburdening them. The counselor is often the first person who has the strength to hear the unemployed person's pain. When the unemployed person is given time to grieve, he or she can move beyond depression to acceptance of the loss. Only then is he or she ready to create a new life.

If the layoff notice was sudden, without prior announcement, the individual may experience a period of numbness, disbelief, and partial denial.[6] In fact, unemployment insurance and other compensations can protract the denial and interfere with the unemployed person's realization of loss, so that the person does not acutely experience the loss of function until unemployment benefits run out. Perhaps this phenomenon explains why the project staff see more people who have been unemployed for almost a year--their benefits are about to run out. While still receiving benefits, the unemployed person's ability to provide for his or her family is still evidenced, and his or her role as breadwinner remains intact. Frequently, when presenting problems are given, unemployment is not even reported. Clients usually present marital difficulties, problems with children, psychosomatic ailments, and other problems that are associated with anxiety and depression.

Almost immediately, upon loss or anticipation of loss, a person gets panicky, restless, agitated, and frightened. He or she may have headaches, sleep problems, or other physiological accompaniments of anxiety. For example, Ms. F, a forty-seven-year-old, white, divorced female called the agency complaining of intense headaches and a need to live on a reduced income by herself. Ms. F had been laid off for approximately seven months and had moved in with her twenty-five-year-old daughter. The daughter recently announced that she was planning to marry. Ms. F stated that she was just beginning to recover from her job loss, which had stimulated severe headaches. As the counselor connected job loss and anticipatory loss of her daughter with her headaches, the client became less distressed.

One of the more prominent and dramatic reactions to loss is the urge to search for and find the object which has been lost. The unemployed person is preoccupied with the loss. His or her thoughts and activities are obsessed by it, which may limit his or her ability to perceive the total job picture objectively. He or she has a heightened awareness of certain clues and is oblivious to other important aspects of the hunt.

Some unemployed people may be preoccupied with identifying a certain kind of potential job and spend hours perusing want ads, circling certain ads. Yet they may not apply or else may apply several days later. Others may be so intent on getting job interviews that they apply for inappropriate jobs or go to interviews unprepared. One person rushed to an interview in dirty, disheveled clothing, only to discover he had not noticed a part of the job description which specifically excluded him.

The frenzied activities of unemployed persons who are incessantly engaged in inappropriate job searches have been frequently observed. They are a tremendous frustration to family members. Usually, these unemployed people do not lack intelligence or knowledge about how to find jobs. They lack the calm acceptance of their state that enables them to use their intelligence and knowledge effectively.

Anger and guilt are also manifestations of a grief reaction. The anger may be directed outward to those who prematurely confront the bereaved person with the loss. The guilt may be directed inward toward self when a person regards his or her job loss as due to personal deficiency. The unemployed person may vacillate between morbid self-blame for all possible inadequacies and bursts of anger against whomever may be around. For example, Mrs. S, a thirty-year-old white mother of two children, came to the agency because of alleged child abuse. Mrs. S's marriage to an alcoholic man had been difficult. Since her husband was unable to keep a job, she maintained stable employment as a seamstress for one of the auto companies. The downturn in car sales resulted in her being laid off. Although her job loss occurred almost a year before, her anger over the loss was still intense. She felt helpless and out of control. She felt inadequate as a parent. While she was employed, her husband assumed major parenting responsibilities. Now she was expected to assume that role. During a stressful period, Mrs. S lost control of her anger and struck her daughter. She was reported by her mother-in-law for suspected child abuse.

Mrs. S recounted many somatic difficulties--increased appetite, increased sleeping, lethargy, and feelings of low self-regard. Mrs. S's job was a means to her independence and competency.

Unemployed persons will frequently describe their

feelings of loss in violent, physical terms, evoking feelings of mutilation and loss of self. The symbols and behaviors representative of one's employment are internalized and become a part of one's identity. Symbols with which people may identify include licenses and degrees, uniforms, and badges. Nameplates, desks, typewriters, and other tools of the trade may psychologically become a part of the person. The unemployed person may want and need to hold onto these symbols in order to maintain his or her own sense of intactness, enabling him or her to recognize and accept the loss. For example, Mrs. T, a thirty-five-year-old married black woman, came to the agency complaining of spouse abuse. She had been laid off from a small medical lab five months before. This had been her first job since the birth of her youngest child. In the treatment group for the unemployed, she shared her experience of being notified of the layoff. She recalled that everyone was at work that day--supervisors, lab assistants, technicians. The word had been going around earlier in the week that there would be layoffs, but no one knew who or when. The notifications began Thursday morning with telephone calls to the various departments. Everyone was on "pins and needles" and in pain, awaiting the piercing ring of the telephone that would direct the employee to the personnel office. It was approximately 3:30 p.m. when the telephone rang for her. She felt stabbed, wounded, and numb as she walked down the corridor to the personnel office. The corridor was deathly dark and long; time seemed to stand still. Her heart was pounding loudly with fear. She entered the personnel office and the personnel director said, "I'm sorry, but . . ." She heard very little afterwards, except, "Mrs. T., return your lab coat and identification badge to the clerk." The reclaiming and repossession of her lab coat and badge was the final assault. She angrily tore them off and threw them on the floor, fleeing home without seeming to breathe or see anything. She felt she had been violated and mutilated. The next morning she remembered lying in bed, wanting to get up at the designated waking hour, but remembering, painfully, that she didn't have to work anymore. Throughout the day, she would look at the clock for breaktime and tug at her chest where the badge would be just as she would do at work.

"You know," she said, "I have never talked with anyone about these feelings because I thought they were peculiar."

Douglas H. Powell and Paul F. Driscoll[7] have identified four stages that the unemployed middle-class professional person experiences. There is initially a "period of relaxation and relief" as the anxiety of waiting for the ax to fall is gone. After a rest period, the person will enter the "period of concerted effort," where he or she will energetically look for work. When these efforts do not pay off and the person is still unemployed, a "period of vacillation and doubt" sets in and mood changes occur. If this continues long enough and the person does not gain employment, he or she enters the "period of malaise and cynicism."

Malaise and cynicism are frequently results of unresolved grief. Many people have been taught to deny feelings that are associated with grief. Feelings related to grief are so forbidden, disturbing, and unfamiliar that the person may indeed feel as though he or she is going crazy. A few may experience psychotic depression. For example, Mr. J had been an unusually competent worker in a high-status trade for twenty-eight years before his company collapsed. He had a loving family, but he tended to keep to himself. He worked long hours, was quiet, and not too involved with the family. He had many associates, but no close friends. His job was his major identity. After his unemployment benefits ran out, his family noticed inappropriate behavior; he worried excessively. He focused on the furnace--he wore his coat in the house and expressed fear that the furnace would break down.

His family thought a job would snap him out of his condition. They were delighted when a former co-worker offered him a temporary job. But the morning he was to start work, he completely collapsed--he could not function, he could hardly talk. He had to be hospitalized with psychotic depression.

Some unemployed people may experience the loss as a devastating blow to a sense of self. Others experience the loss as a relatively mild discomfort. There are those who move from the experience of relief (Powell and Driscoll's first stage) to acceptance of their situation with relatively little need to grieve the loss. What accounts for the nature of the response, its direction, and magnitude may be related to the attachment established between the person and his or her employment.

Four elements of the person's attachment to his or her employment which affect the magnitude of the grief reaction to job loss are: (1) notification procedure, (how and when notified), (2) security of employment, (3) involvement-commitment to the work, and (4) informal and formal support systems.

ASSESSMENT VARIABLES

People confronted with unemployment do not react in identical ways. In order to assess the impact of unemployment on individuals and families, certain variables need to be considered.

It is essential to evaluate where clients are in the grieving process. Their grief will color all other aspects of their lives. If a client is acutely depressed, the depression must be handled. The assessment of the client will be different if the depression is reactive to the job loss rather than another cause. The client's mental health before the job loss needs assessment. Whatever problems the person had while working will probably be exacerbated if he or she loses work. If there were problems with self-esteem prior to job loss, self-esteem may worsen. If there was a healthy self-image, the person may be able to maintain it providing he or she develops effective coping mechanisms.

An employment history is essential to the assessment. What kind of work has been done in the past? Is the client new to the problems of unemployment or has he or she been in this situation before? How has the client coped with unemployment in the past? Where unemployment is a chronic problem, there may be more need for vocational counseling in addition to treatment, as the reason for unemployment may be more than the recession.

What are the internal resources that an individual can draw on? Some questions to bear in mind while assessing a client's resources are: How bright and imaginative is this person? What has the person tried to do already? Does the person have enough ego strength to look for odd jobs now to tide him or her over? Is there a skill or resource that the person has discounted because of low self-esteem? What are the formal support systems the unemployed person can and will avail her or himself of? What financial supports can be used? The worker needs to be informed about eligibility requirements for the various formal financial supports like unemployment insurance and public assistance. Information regarding the person's attitude toward accepting financial help is crucial. Some people refuse to apply for public assistance even though they are eligible.

In addition to formal financial supports, available formal job finding supports need to be considered. Can private or pubic employment agencies be used? Is a referral to a vocational counseling agency to get assistance with job search skills warranted? Being knowledgeable about the availability and affordability of training and retraining programs is also helpful.

What informal support network is available to the unemployed person? Louis A. Ferman and Mary C. Blehar studied unemployed people in Detroit during the mid-1970s. They concluded that "The family--nuclear and extended--(is) the principal source of sustained emotional and functional support for the unemployed."[8] The amount of familial support available and the ability of the person to request such support are important variables to be explored. Some unemployed people try to protect their families from the burden of depression. Therefore, counselors' offices may be the only places where they can show their true feelings.

Age is an important variable. Older unemployed persons appear to suffer more severe emotional stress than their younger counterparts. Some firms have exerted pressure on older employees to retire early as a cost-saving measure. When older people compete with younger people for jobs, the employer may favor the younger person who may have less financial responsibility and be more willing to accept less income. An older prospective employee may be looked on as someone who has fewer years to give to a job and therefore not as profitable an investment, considering the cost of the training period. An employer does not want to hire a person and immediately have to consider providing retirement benefits. An employer may hire a younger person if he or she thinks that older people will take more sick leave than younger people.

Race is an important variable. Despite affirmative action and equal opportunity employment, it is still particularly difficult for minorities to find jobs. They are often the last hired and first fired.

Certain family situations may create additional stress for the unemployed. For example, single parents may have difficulty affording child care while looking for jobs. Are there available resources? A single parent is often caught in the welfare trap of wanting to work but discovering that with each step forward another benefit is cut, making it seem as if one is going backwards by working. Timely information, planning, and extra emotional support from counselors may enable such clients to move ahead.

The current family pattern must be explored as well as the pattern which existed during times of employment. The more role changes there are for a person to adjust to, the higher the stress level. There are a host of possible role changes: Has the person had to move back in with his or her parents? Becoming dependent after having achieved independence is quite a blow. If a whole family has to move back into the parental home, the strain can be even worse. Is Grandmother doing all the parenting now? Has a wife had to find a job for the first time in her married life when her husband is laid off? Does the unemployed husband become the primary child-care provider for the first time in his life? Not only do the loss of a job and having his wife work make him feel inadequate, but new responsibility without preparation will compound these feelings. The unemployed man may take over tasks that the wife considers her territory and she may develop resentment over her loss. A person's identity is linked with his or her job. When the job is lost, the person also loses the identity and specific role he or she derived from the workplace.

The counselor must help the client and his or her family appreciate the validity of their suffering.

Many people tend to regard employment as only a means to a paycheck. However, one's job is a major component in one's identity. The job provides structure around which people build their lives. The job provides social outlets. For many people, the job provides a major target for expression of hostility and aggression. Experts believe that the greatest tragedy for a woman is widowhood, and for a man, job loss.[9] The community expects a person to be upset after the death of a spouse. But neither the community nor the individual may consider grief necessary after losing a job as long as he or she receives unemployment benefits.

TREATMENT

Early in the treatment, the counselor needs to help the client recognize the relationship between the presenting problem and unemployment. It may be necessary for the counselor just to sit with a client for a considerable time. The client may need to be brought through numbness to talk about his or her loss. The client may need to tell the story repeatedly as he or she gains new perspectives. The counselor offers support and encouragement during this period. The client may profit from being told that he or she is not alone, that the layoff is not a personal failure.

Of course, the tangible needs of families must be addressed. Sometimes it is essential to provide clients with food before even considering emotional conditions. Other clients may not be able to follow through with plans to attend to tangible needs until they have been helped past numbness or suicidal depression.

As clients move along in resolving their grief, attention is shifted to day-to-day functioning. Clients are encouraged to maintain themselves physically and emotionally. The counselor needs to help unemployed people put structure into their lives to replace the structure which work provided. Exercise is important. Physical activity is a good way to dispel anxiety. Clients are urged to plan pleasant experiences. Areas of the clients' lives which are going well are underscored and built upon. The clients' attention is turned to ways in which they have overcome obstacles in the past.

In order to mobilize a client's energy, it may be important that something positive begin to happen relating to employment. If an unemployed person can get even some small job, self-esteem may be enhanced, and a sense of helplessness may be reduced. He or she may be elevated back into the provider role in the family. A sense of purpose and accomplishment will thereby be promoted. The previous family homeostasis may be regained.

Each client brings a unique set of strengths and weaknesses to the agency. Unemployment becomes one important issue among other important issues in the total picture of the client. It is necessary to develop a good therapeutic relationship. As in all treatment cases, the therapist must be accepting, understanding, and nonjudgmental. Clients must be able to make decisions for themselves.

Once clients have overcome the worst of their depression, counselors may introduce specific job-seeking assistance. Counselors may help clients write resumes. In the process, they can be helped to review their history in such a way as to recognize strengths, to attain an enhanced sense of personal identity, and to realistically assess where they might be able to fit into the job market.

Clients need help in perceiving unemployment as a unique opportunity for growth. The old homeostasis is disrupted; positive changes can be made before the family settles into a new homeostasis.

Old, unresolved conflicts may emerge around the crisis of unemployment. These conflicts can be reviewed, lived through, and more successfully resolved. For example, Mr. P, a thirty-two-year-old black single male, lost his computer job six months previously. It had been his fourth job since receiving his master's degree six years before. He had either been fired, asked to resign, or laid off. The current job loss was due to an "involuntary" resignation. More important was the aftermath of the job loss, resulting in Mr. P's reassessing his career choice, skills, interests, and life functioning. This review had been too painful before, due to the psychic and educational investment he had placed in his learning. With the aid of therapy, Mr. P came to realize that his current choice and subsequent investment in his career were related to the fear that he would end up at his father's garage as a mechanic, like his younger brother. His resistance to becoming a mechanic was related to his feelings of being imprisoned, held hostage by his father (father's profession). He wanted to be free of the father. His fight for emancipation was uncovered in therapy and, consequently, for the first time in his life, he felt liberated, able to do what he wanted, not governed by what he didn't want to do. The reworking of the developmental phase of emancipation, coming to terms with the past and more recent work experiences, and reworking issues stimulated by the loss, created an opportunity for Mr. P to grow and develop a new and improved relationship with work. Some people will seemingly never again regain paid employment that provides the life-style to which they were previously accustomed. Their grief may, therefore, be more extensive. When they can accept this loss, they are able to develop a new and satisfying life-style.

IMPACT ON COUNSELORS

Mental health professionals are constantly at risk for burnout. Working with the unemployed presents unusual problems. The fact that the counselor is employed and the client is not may create uncomfortable feelings. The counselor may feel guilty that he or she has a job. With curtailment in the mental health fields, most counselors have some sense of vulnerability to the loss of their own jobs. A counselor may, therefore, have special difficulties maintaining an empathic-objective relationship with an unemployed client. Counselors may deny the problem and not be empathic or they may overidentify with clients and lose objectivity.

Counselors may feel inadequate when they cannot help clients get the resources they need to keep food on the table and heat in the house. They may compound this feeling with a sense of guilt about being better off than their clients and may want to give more than they realistically can.

Although family counselors know they are not responsible for obtaining jobs for their clients, they may still feel as if they are. Counselors who may not consider their treatment successful until the client has a job may not be able to help clients cope with the stresses of their current lives.

Counselors must attend to their own mental health in order to be available to their unemployed clients. They need supervisors who can "hear" their upset and help them regain perspective. They need support from colleagues. They need to share with each other ways they have been able to serve unemployed clients effectively. Above all, they need to take care of themselves by maintaining a balance of healthy diversions in order to feel relaxed and reduce anxiety. They need to nourish themselves so that they have sufficient energy to work effectively. Burnout is not from too much work; it is from the negative feelings that are attached to the work. If therapists feel ineffective, inadequate, and tired, burnout will occur more quickly.

REFERENCES

1. United States Department of Labor, Bureau of Labor Statistics, Washington, D.C., April 1982.

2. *Michigan Labor Market Review* (Detroit: Job Service, Michigan Employment Security Commission, April 1982), p. 4.

3. Statistics provided by the Research Department of the United Community Services of Metropolitan Detroit.

4. John Hayes and Peter Nutman, *Understanding the Unemployed* (London and New York: Tavistock, 1981).

5. Colin Murray Parks, *Bereavement* (New York: International Universities Press, 1972).

6. Robert A. Cooke, Thomas D. Taber, and Jeffrey T. Walsh, "Developing a Community-Based Program for Reducing the Social Impact of Plant Closing," *Journal of Applied Behavioral Science*, 15 (February 1979), 133-55.

7. Douglas H. Powell and Paul F. Driscoll, "Middle-Class Professionals Face Unemployment," *Society* 10 (January-February 1973); 18-26.

8. Louis A. Ferman and Mary C. Blehar, "Family Adjustment to Unemployment," in *Families Today* (Washington D.C.: National Institute of Mental Health Monograph, 1979), p. 422.

9. Robert C. Atchley, *The Social Forces in Later Life* (Miami, Florida: Scripts Foundation Grant Center, Miami University, 1977), pp. 212, 215.

APPENDIX 2

THE TRAUMA OF UNEMPLOYMENT AND ITS CONSEQUENCES*

BY JOSEPH F. MADONIA

Economic activity in almost all of the United States has been adversely affected by the prolonged economic decline in manufacturing and housing as well as by cutbacks in government employment. The 10.1 percent unemployment figure reported for September 1982 was the first since 1941 to reach the double digit level. This percentage means that 11.3 million workers were jobless, the highest number since the Great Depression.[1]

Michigan, which depends largely on the auto industry, had the highest unemployment rate with 15.9 percent in September 1982 according to the Bureau of Labor Statistics. Some communities in Michigan reported unemployment at 24 percent. A figure of 24.3 percent was recorded in Gallatin, a small county in Illinois.[2] In Oregon, the recession is severe because of the slump in forest products, related to cutbacks in housing starts. Oregon, with unemployment of 10.3 percent, ranked eighteenth among the fifty states.[3]

---

*From Social Casework: The Journal of Contemporary Social Work 7 (October 1983): 482-88.

Unemployment rates in some areas of the Sun Belt are the highest since statistics have been kept. Even in relatively prosperous energy-producing sectors--such as Oklahoma and Texas--jobs have been cut because of the slide in oil prices and the curtailment of construction. The Texas Employment Commission reported that Houston had 1,135 job listings in September 1982, down from 3,252 a year earlier.[4] Figures from the Bureau of Labor Statistics showed that from September 1981 to September 1982 unemployment in the Dallas-Fort Worth area increased from 4.9 percent to 6.4 percent and Texas unemployment statewide increased from 5.4 percent to 8.4 percent.[5] A growing number of Sun Belt states have qualified for extended federal unemployment benefits.[6]

STATISTICS ARE PEOPLE

The statistics tell only one side of the story. Each statistic is composed of people, many of whom are facing prolonged unemployment for the first time in their careers. A variety of feelings are aroused as a result of being laid off. Not only individuals but families are affected. This suggests that social agencies should program help for such individuals and families, specifically directed at preventing and resolving the emotional problems created by prolonged unemployment.

As recession grows, so does the ripple effect of each layoff or threatened layoff. More people than those who actually lose their jobs are affected. In varying degrees, unemployment also affects their families, friends, co-workers, and neighbors. A small town suffers from a plant closing if a large portion of its economy depends on the workers employed there.[7] The effect ripples through every business in town, touching retailers, small enterprises, and professional services. Laborers suffer because the demand for housing and new construction diminishes.

While the burden of joblessness still falls most heavily on blue collar workers, it is being shared by the ranks of white collar employees.[8] Layoffs are especially severe for skilled workers because they can't find jobs that will pay the same high wages many of them had earned. Recession creates many acute problems which last long beyond economic recovery. Even when an upswing appears, it will be months, even years, before the employment picture returns to normal. Many economists contend unemployment will stay in the 7 percent to 8 percent range well into 1984.[9]

A STUDY OF THE JOBLESS

This article is based on a study undertaken to learn how unemployed workers cope with long-term joblessness. It looks at the effects unemployment has on those who have worked most of their lives. The study focused on thirty men and five women who had an average employment history of ten years in white collar, skilled, and unskilled positions. The study population was representative of many Americans who have been accustomed to work but suddenly find themselves out of jobs and with little prospect of finding others in the immediate future.

The study was conducted in Los Angeles. Cooperation in locating subjects came from a private organization that assists unemployed management and professional persons. Participants were selected who were willing to undergo an intensive interview involving much personal information. All of them were over twenty-one years of age, most were middle-aged. They were typical working-class and middle-class Americans who had worked an average of ten years in their skill area or profession. Some had been employed as long as twenty years in one position.

Interviews were conducted by researchers trained

in the behavioral sciences. The interview schedule for the study was based on a questionnaire designed in collaboration with an aerospace corporation that had experienced several large-scale layoffs during the last several years. The interviews concentrated on exploring psychosocial reactions to unemployment. These were uncovered by questions about reactions to stress and items measuring affective and cognitive responses. There were also questions about the worker's family and significant interpersonal relationships. One of the recurring problems in unemployment is the damaging effect it has on self-esteem. Several questions were constructed to measure the relationship of joblessness to self-image.

The worst jolt to the worker is the notification of the layoff. This arouses feelings of loss because, for many workers, their whole lives are tied up with jobs.[10] For those who have been with one company for most of their adult life, a layoff is a profound shock even if it was expected. The job and the company are so closely related to their identity that the first reaction is one of crisis. This is particularly true when there are few other jobs in sight and they must vie for positions for which hundreds of others may be in competition.

The white collar or blue collar worker's most immediate concern is finding another job and making ends meet on less income. At first, the unemployed person with savings is equipped to deal with the tangible aspects of the situation, but prolonged joblessness is a major concern. The combination of dissipating savings and no job prospects is devastating to a worker, not only financially but also because it creates anxieties about the prospect of having to apply for public assistance after unemployment benefits run out; workers consider this the last step in a downward economic and social spiral.

White collar workers, thrown out of work for the first time, are permanently affected. Harold G. Kaufman found that once professionals have experienced a period of unemployment, their self-esteem is reduced regardless of how successful they are in obtaining work.[11] Professional and white collar workers suffer from the anguish of not being able to pay bills and provide for their families; changing careers is hard. Retooling is easier for blue collar workers than it is for professionals who often have to start at the beginning. This is a grim prospect when there is no assurance that they will find new jobs, even if they can afford to train for new professions.

Although unskilled workers have a different attachment to their work than professionals do, to be laid off by a company they have been with for most of their lives creates a sense of loss. Identity is tied to jobs. The routine schedule--7:00 a.m. to 4:00 p.m., five days a week--is a structure no longer available to them. At first, some express relief: "I never liked the job" and "It's good to get a fresh start." Paramount attention is given to finding new employment and the value of being productive, but when there is no prospect of work, the blue collar worker suffers tremendously from idleness.

Self-esteem is affected by prolonged unemployment.[12] Almost all of the participants reported having felt discouraged about their capabilities because of unemployment: "It makes me feel lousy about myself at times." When asked, "What does it feel like to be out of work?" interviewees responded with terms like "not contributing," "useless," "a failure," and "worthless." Others reported such affective responses as depression and anxiety. Cognition was also affected; confusion and disorganization were reported. Twenty-three percent of the respondents expressed feelings of pessimism and anger.

Although the workers did not blame themselves for the loss of their jobs, 70 percent reported feeling badly about themselves. This was related to the idleness of the jobless. Without day-to-day accomplishments, people accustomed to work and the psychological gratifications it offers feel insecure and inadequate. Dependency increases and autonomy diminishes. Self-esteem is significantly affected and the basis for depression is established. Without the objective reinforcement of self-worth, a vicious cycle of self-degradation occurs in a great many of the unemployed, even when it is obvious to them that they had nothing to do with the job losses.

The job had been the axis along which the pattern of the respondents' lives were organized. Work served to maintain the person in a social group, structure life activity, and determine social participation. The loss of the job meant not only loss of income; there is a significant meaning to work, and without it many difficulties ensue.[13]

EFFECTS ON THE FAMILY

Attention in the interviews was given to examining the impact of joblessness on family members. Loss of a job by the breadwinner created anxieties. Over half of the thirty-five participants reported that unemployment was significantly upsetting their families. Most reported that, at first, unemployment drew the family closer together to work on common goals and provide mutual support. The coming together occurred almost immediately following the notice of the layoff. The crisis at hand tied the group together, a phenomenon first recorded by Emile Durkheim.[14] This was a natural and common response to crisis. But in all cases, the family support did not last.

The victim of the layoff was very desirous of receiving understanding and support from his or her spouse. When it was not available, the unemployed person felt more estranged from the family and blamed himself or herself for the problems caused by loss of income. The sense of estrangement had repercussions in family interaction. Arguments increased with spouses and children; over one-third of the respondents reported an increase in the frequency of arguments with spouses following unemployment.

Redistribution of wage-earning responsibility within a family resulted in a readjustment of role expectations. Tension in the family rose and general disharmony occurred. Clearly, love and family support are critical for the victim of joblessness; without them major difficulties follow.[15]

The loss of income caused disruptions in the family's social relationships. The depletion of financial resources reduced contact with relatives and friends because of the inability to reciprocate social obligations. Due to reduced income, many people withdrew from social activities, clubs, recreational and political groups.[16] This cut down social interaction and eliminated sources of recreation and other stress-reducing activities.

In most cases, the families which were intact emotionally, socially, and financially prior to the unemployment of the main breadwinner rode out the storm; only occasionally did the psychological and financial pressures build to an unbearable level. These were not the families at risk. The families at risk were those who reported previous problems in regard to finances, health, and marital relationships. The shock of unemployment drew the families together but only for a brief period of time. Without a solution to the problem, and with continuing financial difficulties, relationships became strained, nonsupportive, and disruptive. Problems that were in the open prior to the layoff became exacerbated. Those bubbling below the surface emerged into conflict. In the absence of an outside mediator, the situation often deteriorated; without outside support, many of these families came apart at the time members needed each other the most. The findings of this study are evidence in support of the need for family assistance for the unemployed. The data also corroborate findings reported previously by Ruth Cavan, Mira Komarovsky, and Sol Ginsburg.

EFFECTS ON SOCIAL RELATIONSHIPS

Unemployment created a new role in social relationships for people who were previously productive and self-sufficient. The socially useful role associated with work, which gave the individual a sense of identity, was missing. Being unemployed signified a loss of autonomy, especially when the unemployment continued and the worker had little hope of a job. Respondents reported a desire to share their concerns and anxieties with someone they knew.

Although strengthened by the sympathy and help of others, the unemployed suffered a dilemma. Emotional support was helpful in coping with stress, but the dependency it engendered became alarming. They didn't like to rely on others since this reminded them of their nonproductiveness. Seventy-four percent of those interviewed reported spending more time alone, and 67 percent experienced increased irritability in relations with others. Irritability occurred mainly with spouses and loved ones who expressed a need to offer support. Thirty-four percent of those interviewed declared that they were having more arguments with spouses than they did when employed.

In spite of reported difficulties in getting along with others, those without friends or family to rely on were even more vulnerable to distress.

Socially isolated prior to the layoff, they learned that the increased isolation simply added greater emotional burdens.

PSYCHOLOGICAL REACTIONS

The psychological cost of joblessness became more painful to many victims than the strain of making ends meet. Eighty percent of the thirty-five respondents reported that they were more easily frustrated than when they were employed. Close to 70 percent noted an agitated, tense state which they expected would continue until they found jobs. Three quarters of those interviewed indicated that they worried much more than when the were working. Although worrying can be a form of problem solving, it becomes a problem in itself when no solutions are possible for the person and the jobless status becomes permanent. Signs of emotional depression began to show, compounded by the absence of work and other activity. Although it is important that the unemployed keep busy, that was not always possible.

Half of the thirty-five respondents reported having more trouble falling asleep than when they were working and 37 percent noted crying more frequently. Little things upset them more easily. Forty-four percent of the respondents felt at times as if they just didn't care about anything. A substantial majority of those undergoing anxiety and depression had experienced stress prior to the job loss involving hospitalization, divorce or separation, the death of someone close, or great expense.

Not all of the unemployed suffered. Some reported positive effects: "It gave me a chance to look at myself." Others welcomed "an opportunity to examine where one's been and where one is going" or viewed unemployment as "a way of getting a new start." But for the majority, the prospect of continued joblessness created concerns about money, family, emotional well-being, and physical health.

It has been found that joblessness engenders stress that can aggravate or cause health problems.[17] Stanislov Kasl, Susan Gore, and Sidney Cobb reported that people who remain unemployed do not feel well physically.[18] Twenty percent of those interviewed for the study noted more frequent headaches than when they were working. Three-quarters thought that being out of work was harder on their health than working.

Many found that they could not afford to maintain health insurance with their resources. Some qualified for Medicaid, others simply hoped to remain healthy. They deferred all but the most necessary medical care. Without insurance, private psychotherapeutic treatment was beyond their reach, yet 29 percent of the participants stated that they could have benefited from personal counseling. They also reported that job counseling, more education, and job training would have been helpful.

A NEED FOR ACTION

Each new layoff brings a sharp rise in the number of people seeking help for family disturbances or emotional problems related to a recession. When depressed economic opportunity continues unabated, unemployment creates serious psychological consequences. Men and women suffer a sharp loss of self-esteem, a diminished sense of identity, a sense of estrangement from friends, and a feeling of being left out. Problems are even greater and dissolution of the marriage or separation often occur in cases where unemployment was preceded by marital or family conflict.

The social costs of unemployment will have long-term effects; repercussions will continue long after the recession is over. Sensible social policy must be promoted which restores work immediately. Work is a significant part of an individual's existence and opportunities must be provided for full employment.

Social agencies must take a leadership role in assisting the unemployed in their communities. Many of today's unemployed have not needed assistance in the past and are not familiar with social agency programs. Methods of assisting them--including outreach--must be devised by agencies. Outreach has been used by the social work profession since its inception. For the unemployed, this approach is particularly appropriate since it enables an agency to identify potential clients, alert them to the services available, and help them make use of services.[19]

Because many of the unemployed lose contact with their customary social networks, it is critical for social agencies to promote an active outreach program. Services may include the regular programs offered by an agency--family counseling, individual psychotherapy, or financial aid--but for most of the unemployed, the non-financial services of an agency are not appropriate.

One of the first places to reach the unemployed is through the personnel department of the last employer. It is best to contact the worker at the time of layoff and personnel departments will cooperate with social agencies if they are approached. But many of the unemployed quickly lose contact with their former employers. Places where they can be reached vary with the services they seek out and include state employment offices, food stamp offices, and churches and synagogues. More aggressive outreach in communities with long-term unemployment should include locating the unemployed in such neighborhood meeting places as parks, bars, social clubs, and YMCAs.

Social work agencies can be instrumental in promoting self-help groups for the unemployed. Major efforts by the agency could involve recruiting for the group, helping with preliminary organization, advertising the program, and making the agency's physical facilities available for meetings. The agency person who promotes the self-help group can serve as its liaison since agency services frequently become necessary for group members or their families.

In addition to self-help programs, group sessions--with an educative rather than a therapeutic orientation--can be developed by family service agencies, community mental health centers, or the social work staff of state employment or food stamp offices. For example, an agency can designate a staff member to lead a group which concentrates on basic information about the social and psychological consequences of joblessness. A group is a good vehicle for preventive services because it permits an exchange of feelings, ideas, and experiences and reduces the burden of being uncomfortable in the one-to-one relationship with an agency person. It also builds esprit de corps which is vital for the unemployed. The exchange of information and feelings with others in the same position is a good way of breaking the downward psychological spiral and bolstering self-esteem.

Unemployed persons must be helped to understand that decreases in self-esteem and feelings of isolation, dependency, anxiety, and depression are common reactions to stress. They should be educated about the effect joblessness will have on their family relationships. Provisions must also be made to include spouses in some or all of the group sessions. Practical information can also be discuussed in the group about retraining programs in the community, the types of jobs that may be available, the mechanics of changing careers, and how to update or prepare resumes.

Agencies should be creative in developing their programs. Efforts should be made to separate unemployment groups from other services. In promoting a program of this type, it is important to stress the nontherapeutic function of the group.

In communities with unemployment rates of over 20 percent, job searching becomes futile for many. Social agencies can serve the unemployed by offering information abut relocation. As painful as relocation may be for some, they must be encouraged to consider it. Providing relocation information is an involved task, but for many there is no one available whom they can consult. Social agencies must be willing to accept the responsibility. Relocation is costly financially and emotionally, and it should be approached thoughtfully. Practical information can be provided to the families of the unemployed and the emotional burdens involved in leaving familiar surroundings can be discussed with them.

There are still recession proof areas of the country, especially for certain industries. An agency should determine which states and metropolitan regions are best. This information can be obtained from federal agencies such as the Bureau of Economic Analysis (U.S. Department of Commerce), the Bureau of Labor Statistics (U.S. Department of Labor), or the Bureau of the Census. Other resources include the Places Related Almanac published by Rand McNally and relocation planning guides distributed through home equity corporations and relocation services.

Some unemployed persons have the resources to finance their move and establish themselves in a new locality. Others, who need help with the relocation, should be told about the Travelers Aid offices in their new city communities. Information about other social agencies should also be provided.

At first, relocation of a family may not involve all of its members. The wage earner may have to leave the family and establish a financial base before he or she can afford to move the household. In these cases, social agencies should be available to offer supportive services to those left behind.

In addition to doing outreach, sponsoring self-help programs, and offering preventive and relocation services, agencies must also make traditional psychosocial services available. Crisis intervention and short-term psychotherapy may be needed to help with the debilitating symptoms associated with unemployment. The sliding fee arrangements of many agencies make them a natural resource for those who are suffering from the trauma of unemployment yet are no longer covered by insurance.

The study discussed in this article dealt with unemployed people who were looking for work. There is a growing population of "discouraged workers" whom the Bureau of Labor Statistics defines as persons who want to work but cannot find a job and have not looked actively within the past four weeks. The discouraged workers are unskilled, undereducated, and accustomed to long periods of unemployment. Their benefits have run out. Many live in high unemployment areas and have stopped looking for work. Without money or possessions, they are turning to shelters for housing and to charities for food and clothing. The discouraged workers are more needy than the unemployed and one agency cannot serve all their needs. The plight of the discouraged worker, as well as the unemployed, will continue to worsen until sensible social planning occurs.

REFERENCES

1. U.S. Department of Labor, Bureau of Labor Statistics, Employment and Earnings, vol. 29, no. 9 (Washington, DC: U.S. Government Printing Office, September 1982).

2. U.S. Department of Labor, Bureau of Labor Statistics, "State and Metropolitan Area Employment and Unemployment," press release, 19 October 1982.

3. U.S. Department of Labor, Employment and Earnings, vol. 29, no. 9.

4. The Texas Employment Commission, unpublished report (Washington, DC: U.S. Department of Labor, October 1982).

5. U.S. Department of Labor, "State and Metropolitan Area Employment and Unemployment."

6. "Unemployment Insurance Laws: Changes in 1981," Monthly Labor Review 105 (February 1982).

7. Alfred Slote, Termination: The Closing at Baker Plant (Indianapolis, IN: Bobbs-Merrill, 1969).

8. U.S. Department of Labor, Bureau of Labor Statistics, Employment and Earnings, vol. 29, no. 5 (Washington, DC: U.S. Government Printing Office, May 1982).

9. Wall Street Journal, 10 May 1982, p. 3.

10. Donald Tiffany, The Unemployed: A Social Psychological Portrait (Englewood Cliffs, NJ: Prentice-Hall, 1970).

11. Harold G. Kaufman, "Relations Between Unemployment--Reemployment Experience and Self-Esteem Among Professionals," in _Proceedings of the Eighty-First Annual Convention of the American Psychological Association, Montreal, Canada 1973_, vol. 8, no. 8 (Washington, DC: American Psychological Association, 1973).

12. Richard Wilcock and Walter Franke, _Unwanted Workers: Permanent Lay-offs and Long-Term Unemployment_ (London: Free Press of Glencoe, 1962).

13. Eugene Friedman and Robert Havighurst, _The Sociology of Retirement_ (Minneapolis, MN: University of Minnesota Press, 1961).

14. Emile Durkheim, _Suicide_ (New York: Free Press, 1966).

15. See, for example, Ruth Cavan, "Unemployment Crisis of the Common Man," _Marriage and Family Living_ 21 (May 1959): 139-46; Mira Komarovsky, _The Unemployed Man and His Family_ (New York: Basic Books, 1971); and Sol Ginsburg, "What Unemployment Does to People," _American Journal of Psychiatry_ 99 (November 1942): 439-46.

16. Michael Aiken, Louis Ferman, and Harold Sheppard, _Economic Failure, Alienation and Extremism_ (Ann Arbor, MI: University of Michigan Press, 1968).

17. Barbara Dohrenwend and Bruce Dohrenwend, _Stressful Life Events: Their Nature and Effects_ (New York: John Wiley, 1974).

18. Stanislov Kasl, Susan Gore, and Sidney Cobb, "The Experience of Losing a Job," _Psychosomatic Medicine_ 37 (March 1975); 106-22.

19. Ronald Toseland, "Increasing Access: Outreach Methods in Social World Practice," _Social Casework_ 62 (April 1981); 227-39.

APPENDIX 3

SURVEY OF UNEMPLOYMENT SERVICES/PROGRAMS
PROVIDED BY FAMILY SERVICE AGENCIES
IN NORTH AMERICA

Please Return by April 14, 1984

This survey is divided into five sections:

A. Community Information
B. Agency Information
C. Daily Routine Practice of the Agency
D. General Questions
E. Special Service Project of Your Agency

If your agency is not working with unemployed persons at all fill out just this first page. If your agency works with unemployed persons but had no special service project in 1983 to address unemployment answer questions in sections A, B, C, and D. If you have had a special service project in 1983 to address unemployment answer questions in all sections. If you had more than one special service project duplicate the enclosed extra copy of section E.

1. Does your agency provide or work cooperatively to provide services/programs (clinical, concrete, educational or advocacy) to the unemployed?

   YES ______ If YES please complete the enclosed questionnaire and return by April 14, 1984 along with this signed cover sheet to:

   NATIONAL ACADEMY FOR FAMILIES
   SUITE 852
   475 RIVERSIDE DRIVE
   NEW YORK, NY 10115

   NO ______ If NO please sign this sheet and return it immediately to the NATIONAL ACADEMY FOR FAMILIES (see above for address).

Signed ____________________

Title ____________________

Agency ____________________

Address ____________________

____

SECTION A
COMMUNITY INFORMATION

1. ______ What is the rate of unemployment in the area your agency serves?

2. If possible, please identify up to three service agencies and/or organizations in the area your agency serves which provide the most effective assistance to unemployed persons.

Agency/Organization	Assistance Provided
______________________	______________________
______________________	______________________
______________________	______________________

3. If possible, please identify up to three corporations and/or industries in the area your agency serves which provide the most effective programs/services to assist persons they terminate to prepare for unemployment.

Corporations/Industries	Programs/Services
______________________	______________________
______________________	______________________
______________________	______________________

4. If possible, please identify up to three labor unions in the area your agency serves which provide the most effective programs/services to prepare persons for unemployment and/or to assist unemployed persons.

Labor Unions	Programs/Services
______________________	______________________
______________________	______________________
______________________	______________________

5. Circle the number on the scale which indicates the relative ease or difficulty with which your agency collaborates/interacts with other community service agencies and/or organizations when working on the issue of unemployment.

Easy Collaboration & Interaction (No Turf Problems)	← 1 2 3 4 5 6 7 8 9 10 →	Extremely Difficult Collaboration & Interaction (Many Turf Problems)

6. If you circled any number 6 through 10 please state the major reason for the difficulty in collaboration/interaction.

SECTION B
AGENCY INFORMATION

1. How many years has your agency been in existence? ________

2. What was the total number of clients served by your agency in 1983? ______

3. Please indicate what percentage of clients served in 1983 were in the following family income groups: (Estimate if necessary)

   $10,000 and under ________%
   $10,001 - $15,000 ________%
   $15,001 - $20,000 ________%
   $20,001 and over ________%

4. What percentage of total paid staff time was spent in 1983 on the following: (Estimate if necessary)

   ________% All Clinical Services
   ________% All Community Educational Services
   ________% All Concrete Services
   ________% All Advocacy Services

   (Please answer the above question even if you have no exclusively community educational, concrete service or advocacy staff)

5. Did your agency have paid staff working exclusively on programs/services (including advocacy) for the unemployed in 1983?

   _____ YES On a full-time basis. _____ How many?
   _____ YES On at least a one-half time basis. _____ How many?
   _____ YES On at least a one-quarter time basis. _____ How many?
   _____ NO

6. If you answered YES to either in question number 5 please indicate:

   Credentials (degrees, certification, etc.) ____________________
   ____
   ____

7. Please indicate what percentage of total paid staff time was spent in 1983 on the following: (Estimate if necessary)

   ________% Clinical services to the unemployed
   ________% Community education services to the unemployed
   ________% Concrete services to the unemployed
   ________% Advocacy services for the unemployed

8. If your agency does advocacy what form(s) does it take?

   _____ Legislative
   _____ Legal
   _____ Other (please describe) ____________________________

9. ________% What percentage of total 1983 budget was spent for programs/services to the unemployed (clinical, community education, concrete and advocacy)?

SECTION C

DAILY ROUTINE PRACTICE OF THE AGENCY

(This section deals with your agency's daily routine practice as contrasted with special project(s) or community coalition involvement.)

1. _____ How many routine practice clients (not clients funded or serviced by special service project(s)) did your agency serve in 1983?

2. _____ How many routine practice clients (not clients funded or serviced by special project(s)) who used your agency in 1983 had problems/needs engendered by unemployment? (Estimate if necessary)

3. Of the routine practice clients serviced by your agency in 1983 with problems/needs engendered by unemployment please indicate the number and percentage of: (Estimate if necessary)

	Number	Percent
The unemployed person	_____	_____%
Another family member	_____	_____%

4. Of the routine practice cases in 1983 engendered by unemployment please indicate the number and percentage initially presenting the problem/needs: (Estimate if necessary)

	Number	Percent
The unemployed person	_____	_____%
Another family member	_____	_____%

5. Please indicate the most common clinical problems engendered by unemployment of your 1983 routine practice clients by rank ordering the following problems with #1 being the most common.

____ Family (tension and/or breakdown other than the list below)
____ Personal (stress, depression, anxiety, loss of esteem, grief, anger, blame, confusion, etc.)
____ Role Adjustments
____ Relocation/Separation
____ Drug Abuse
____ Alcohol Abuse
____ Child Abuse
____ Spouse Abuse
____ Suicidal Tendencies
____ Other: ______________________________
____ Other: ______________________________

6. Please indicate the most common service needs engendered by unemployment of your 1983 routine practice clients by rank ordering the following needs with #1 being the most common.

____ Stress Management Training
____ Financial Counseling (budgeting, etc.)
____ Redefining Vocational Goals
____ Job Search Skills (e.g. locating jobs, resume writing, interview skills)
____ Retraining Assistance
____ Job Referral and Placement
____ Community Resource Assistance (where to find resources)
____ Financial Assistance (fuel, food, clothing, mortgage assistance, etc.)
____ Assistance in Securing Entitlement benefits.
____ Other: ______________________________
____ Other: ______________________________

7. Indicate all the ways your agency responded to your 1983 routine practice clients (not special project nor coalition clients) who had problems/needs engendered by unemployment. Put an X in the appropriate column(s).

	Agency Clinical Services	Agency Educational Services	Agency Concrete Services	Agency Advocacy Services	Clients Referred	Designate To Whom Referred
Family (tension and/or breakdown)						
Personal (stress, depression, anxiety, loss of esteem, grief, anger, blame, confusion, etc.)						
Role Adjustments						
Relocation/Separation						
Drug Abuse						
Alcohol Abuse						
Child Abuse						
Spouse Abuse						
Suicidal Tendencies						
Stress Management Training						
Financial Counseling						
Redefining Vocational Goals						
Job Search Skills (locating jobs, resume writing, interview skills etc.)						
Retraining Assistance						
Job Referral & Placement						
Community Resource Assistance (where to find resources)						
Fuel Assistance (food, clothing, (mortgage assistance)						
Assistance in Securing Entitlement Benefits						
Others:						

7. Of those problems/needs noted in the previous question were there any you believe your agency should have dealt with but for some reason did not?

____ YES ____ NO

8. If the answer to number 9 is YES please list up to three problem/needs and the reason(s) your agency did not deal with them.

Problem/Needs	Reasons
____	____
____	____
____	____

9. When you do intake with a routine practice client who is unemployed or a family member of the unemployed person do you routinely inform them about services for the unemployed?

____ YES ____ NO

10. When an unemployed person (not another family member) presents her/himself to your agency seeking help in the course of your routine practice, what is the agency's procedure for providing assistance? Please state briefly the sequential steps you follow in assisting the unemployed routine practice client.

1. ____ 4. ____

2. ____ 5. ____

3. ____ 6. ____

11. What assistance (with exception of additional staff and funding) is needed to increase the effectiveness of your agency's services to unemployed persons who come to you in the course of your routine practice?

12. In the course of its routine practice in 1983 please indicate how many unemployed persons your agency assisted in: (Estimate if necessary)

____ Securing Employment
____ Entering Training/Retraining programs

13. Comment on the effectiveness of your agency's routine practice in responding to the problems/needs engendered by unemployment.

14. Has your agency developed brochure(s) and/or other informational resource(s) relating to your routine practice with the unemployed and/or their families?

____ YES ____ NO

If YES please return two copies of each with this questionnaire.

SECTION D

GENERAL QUESTIONS

IF YOUR AGENCY HAD SPECIAL SERVICE PROJECT(S) TO THE UNEMPLOYED PLEASE ANSWER QUESTIONS IN SECTION E STARTING ON THE NEXT PAGE BEFORE ANSWERING THE QUESTIONS ON THIS PAGE. BE SURE TO COME BACK TO THIS PAGE WHEN YOU FINISH. Otherwise continue answering the questions on this page.

1. Have any publicly funded (Federal, State, County or City) resources or job training programs made a positive impact on your agency's ability to assist the unemployed either through direct funding or through other resources?

   _______ YES _______ NO

2. If yes please identify the three most effective ones and describe how they made a positive impact:

Identify	Describe
______________________	______________________________
______________________	______________________________
______________________	______________________________

3. In your opinion what are the present five most central issues of concern related to your agencies efforts to service individuals and families being affected by unemployment? (Rank order, # 1 being the greatest concern.)

   1.

   2.

   3.

   4.

   5.

4. In your opinion in the next five years what will be the five most central issues of concern related to your agency's efforts to service individuals and families being affected by unemployment? (Rank order # 1 being the greatest concern.)

   1.

   2.

   3.

   4.

   5.

SECTION E
SPECIAL SERVICE PROJECT OF YOUR AGENCY

(This section deals with a special service project of your agency, either free-standing or as part of a coalition, which services the unemployed.)

1. In addition to its routine practice in 1983 did your agency have a special service project for persons affected by unemployment?
_____ YES _____ NO

If YES skip question number 2 and complete the questionnaire.
If NO answer only question number 2 in this section.

IF YOUR AGENCY HAD MORE THAN ONE SPECIAL SERVICE PROJECT IN 1983 DUPLICATE THE ENCLOSED EXTRA FORM.

2. If your agency did not have a special service project for the unemployed in 1983 but is planning one in 1984, please describe what you expect to do.

IF YOUR AGENCY HAD NO SPECIAL SERVICES PROJECT GO TO THE LAST PAGE & CONTINUE.

3. Was your special service project a part of a community coalition?

_____ YES _____ NO (If NO go to question #5 and continue.)

4. If YES:
   a. Name of the coalition. _______________
   b. Which community agencies and/or organizations are involved? _______________
   c. Which corporations and/or industries are involved? _______________
   d. Which unions are involved? _______________
   e. Which religious bodies are involved? _______________
   f. Who initiated the coalition? _______________
   g. When? _______________
   h. Describe your agency's specific role in the coalition.

5. Describe the average participant of your agency's special service project. (Be more specific than unemployed.)

6. Please profile your agency's 1983 special service project.

   a. Please check which best describes the programs/services:

      _____ Clinical
      _____ Concrete
      _____ Educational
      _____ Advocacy
      _____ Other ______________________________

   b. Describe the programs/services of your special service project.

   c. What specifically did your agency attempt to do for the unemployed through the programs/services of your special service project?

   d. Did you use resource persons from outside the agency?
      YES _____ NO _____

   e. What were their areas of expertise?

   f. Site:
   g. Hours Held:
   h. Life of Project: (Length)
   i. How did the project get initiated?

   j. If there was a key person who initiated the project please give:
      Name ______________________________ Title ______________________________

   k. Under whose direction in the agency did the project exist?
      Name ______________________________ Title ______________________________

l. How much was the budget for the project? $__________

m. How was the project funded?

Source	Amount	Please Specifically Identify
Your Agency	$______	____________
United Way	$______	____________
Corporations	$______	____________
Religious Groups	$______	____________
Private Foundations	$______	____________
City/County Government	$______	____________
State Government	$______	____________
Federal Government	$______	____________
Other	$______	____________

n. How did you publicize the project?
T.V. ___ Radio ___ Newspaper ___ Flyer ___ Other (specify) ___

7. Was the business/industrial sector cooperative or resistant? Comment:

8. Were the labor unions cooperative or resistant? Comment:

9. Do you think the general public identified the special service project as being separate from or different than the agency's routine practice?
_____ YES _____ NO

10. Apart from additional staff and funding was there assistance needed that would have made your project more effective?

11. As a result of the special service project in 1983 indicate how many persons: (Estimate if necessary)

______ Secured Employment
______ Entered Training/Retraining programs

12. Comment on the effectiveness of your special service project in responding to the problems/needs engendered by unemployment?

13. Has your agency developed a brochure and/or informational resource relating to your special service project for the unemployed and families?
_____ YES _____ NO

<u>If YES please return two copies of each with this questionnaire.</u>

Please return to page 6 and answer the GENERAL QUESTIONS if you have not done so.

BIBLIOGRAPHY

Katherine H. Briar, "Lay-Offs and Social Work Intervention," Urban and Social Change Review 16 (Summer 1983).

Katherine H. Briar, "Unemployment: Toward a Social Work Agenda," Social Work 28 (May-June 1983).

Terry F. Buss, F. Stevens Redburn, and Joseph Waldron, Mass Unemployment: Plant Closings and Community Mental Health (Beverly Hills, CA: Sage Publications, 1983).

Greg J. Duncan, with Richard D. Coe, Mary E. Corcoron, Martha A. Hill, Saul D. Hoffman, and James N. Morgan, Years of Poverty, Years of Plenty: The Changing Economic Fortunes of American Workers and Their Families (Ann Arbor, MI: Institute for Sociological Research, 1984).

Louis A. Forman and Mary C. Blehar, "Family Adjustment to Unemployment," Families Today (Washington, DC: National Institute of Mental Health Monograph, 1979).

Thomas Keefe, "The Stress of Unemployment," Social Work 29 (May-June 1984): 264-69.

Ramsay Lion and Paula Rayman, "Health and Social Costs of Unemployment: Research and Policy Considerations," American Psychologist 37 (October 1982).

Phyllis Moen, "Preventing Financial Hardship: Coping Strategies of Families of the Unemployed," in Family Stress, Coping and Social Support, ed. Hamilton I. McCubbin, A.E. Cauble, and J.M. Patterson (Springfield, IL: Charles C. Thomas, 1982).

Phyllis Moen, E.L. Kain, and G.H. Elder, Jr., "Economic Conditions and Family Life: Contemporary and

Historical Perspectives," in American Families and the Economy: The High Costs of Living, ed. Richard R. Nelson and Felicity Skidmore (Washington, DC: National Academy Press, 1983).

Colin Murray Parkes, Studies of Grief in Adult Life (New York: International Universities Press, 1972).

Donald W. Riegle,Jr., "The Psychological and Social Effects of Unemployment," American Psychologist 37 (October 1982).

Linda S. Rosenman, "Unemployment of Women: A Social Policy Issue," Social Work 24 (January 1979).

Michael W. Sherraden, "Chronic Unemployed: A Social Work Perspective," Social Work 30 (September-October 1985).

Robert Sunley, Advocating Today: A Human Service Practitioner's Handbook (New York: Family Service America, 1983).